DON'T JUST FIX IT, IMPROVE IT!
A Journey to the Precision Domain

BOOK 1

- *Learn strategies & tools for organizational evolution*
- *Learn how defects affect bottom line results*
- *Learn how to use the Hero's Journey to build a learning organization*
- *And much, much more!*

By WINSTON P. LEDET,
WINSTON J. LEDET
& SHERRI M. ABSHIRE

DON'T JUST FIX IT, IMPROVE IT!
A Journey to the Precision Domain
By Winston P. Ledet, Winston J. Ledet & Sherri M. Abshire

ISBN 978-0-9825-1631-7
HF022021

© 2012-2021, Reliabilityweb, Inc. All rights reserved.
Printed in the United States of America.

This book, or any parts thereof, may not be reproduced, stored in a retrieval system, or transmitted in any form without the permission of the Publisher.

Opinions expressed in this book are solely the author's and do not necessarily reflect the views of the Publisher.

Publisher: Reliabilityweb.com
Cover art: Ron Dronet

www.reliabilityweb.com
8991 Daniels Center Drive, Suite 105, Fort Myers, FL 33912
Toll Free: 888-575-1245 | Office: 239-333-2500
E-mail: crm@reliabilityweb.com

To all the organizations that are currently struggling through their own Hero's Journey in hopes this story provides the courage and inspiration to complete the journey.

Grateful Acknowledgements

To our friend and colleague, Paul Monus, who provided many insights and offered boundless enthusiasm and support to this project.

A big thank you to Eliyahu Goldratt for writing, *The Goal*, which started this genre of books, and to Steve Thomas for keeping it going with his book, *The Journey to Improved Business Performance*.

Thanks to Sandra Maslow Smith who introduced us to the Hero's Journey, which she called the Heroine's Journey, and also to Charlie Krone who provided the framework for seeing an organization as a socio-technical system by introducing us to the works of John Bennett. It provided our foundation to systems thinking.

To Don Kuenzli, Jim Griffith, John Fackelman, Judy Gilbert, James Schaefer, Doug Parrish, Ed Goedde, Marc Schomerous, Keith Mullins and all the employees of the Lima and Port Arthur refineries who provided the proof and inspiration that lasting Heroic Change is possible.

And a very special thanks to Mark Paich, Tony Cardella, Mark Downing, John Sterman, Peter Senge, Art Kleiner, Vince Flynn, Bill VanHoy, Ed Jones, Dennis Lockstedt, and the members of the DuPont Corporate Maintenance Leadership Team who inspired us and helped create the original computer model that led to the creation of The Manufacturing Game® at DuPont.

To Spiro Maroulis, Joe Kubenka, the late Charles Latino, Bob Latino, Ken Latino, Ron Moore, Bob Baldwin, Terry O'Hanlon, Felicjan Rydzak, Andrew Fraser, Rob Jackson, Bob Williamson, Mark Heffernan, Stu Teffeteller, Michel Deveix, John Lightcap, David Burns, Gary Pelini, Dale Blann, Dan Merchant, Larry McVay, Janet Weiss, Jane Linder, Dave Golson, Hal McGaughey, Warren Burgess, and Walter Jones, who helped to make this book possible by providing their knowledge, insights, encouragement and support throughout the many years of research and modeling to prove our theories about Heroic Change.

To Michelle Ledet Henley, who provided the organizational capability, professionalism, and systems to perpetuate our workshops long enough for us to realize the nature of the Hero's Journey and what it takes to complete one.

To June Ledet, who kept the Ledet family together through the entire ordeal of creating a family business and who keeps us in touch with all of our clients.

Foreword

Winston Ledet – A Guide

After a career spanning thirty years in various parts of the maintenance and reliability community, I am amazed at what appears to be a lack of innovation in the implementation of strategies and techniques for driving improved reliability performance that hopefully leads to improved organizational performance.

There are a host of approaches to physical asset management, including Reliability Centered Maintenance, PM Optimization, Total Productive Maintenance and Predictive Condition Based Maintenance. I have witnessed each of these approaches working with various degrees of success and failure. Most of the strategies, techniques, and technologies have been available for several decades, and all have documented case studies to demonstrate the technical and business results they generate. That said, research at Reliabilityweb.com documents reliability improvement initiative implementation failures running as high as 80%, even when using these documented methodologies.

Over the course of my slow gathering of knowledge, I have often had the privilege to see Winston Ledet in person, and more often read his work. Each time I sit in on one of his conference presentations, or read one of his articles, I leave with at least one new book to read and a plethora of new ideas. The books are rarely directly related to improving industrial machinery, or even process reliability. They are research reports and books by leading thinkers who study and report on human learning, behaviors, and organizational improvements. He is one of the rare individuals actively guiding us to new and exciting possibilities that exist outside the maintenance and reliability community.

When I first founded the Reliabilityweb.com network, I sat in on a Maintenance Benchmarking presentation delivered by Winston Ledet. It outlined the accomplishments of the Dupont organization in the area of maintenance performance, and it turned out that Winston was part of the team that created those results. The entire maintenance community studied the Dupont benchmarks, and many organizations set out to reach the same performance levels. In the years that followed, you rarely sat in on a presentation that did not reference that benchmarking performance information.

Even after creating such great results, one got the sense that Winston was not satisfied and was searching for a way to recreate, or even enhance, those results in different organizations. He was searching for the keys that would allow any organization that was willing to do what was necessary reach a much higher performance level. He had come to realize that what worked in one location, even in the same company, rarely translated to another location in the same way.

Winston is a great teacher, but that does not do enough to describe what he brings to the maintenance and reliability community. He is also an extraordinary guide who takes us on field trips to new ways of seeing things.

It was like a lightning bolt had struck when I heard Winston state that it took him over twenty years to actually understand what a group of Japanese manufacturing engineers had really meant when they told him about driving defects from the process.

His "Time for you to leave the temple, Grasshopper" moment of enlightenment had arrived.

I could almost hear the sands of time combining with all of Winston's work involving thousands of people and dozens of significant authors to form an approach that seemed elusive because it was so simple at its very core. I heard Winston speaking in a new way that we might all be able to access.

In several follow up conversations, I became even more convinced that Winston could guide many of us to a new way of approaching improved reliability performance. When he mentioned that he had an idea for a fictional account that reflected the central concepts, I jumped in with both feet and encouraged him to complete the work and that we would gladly publish and promote it around the world.

He returned to Texas and, with the able assistance of Sherri Abshire and Winston J. Ledet, created what I consider to be one of the most important works in a decade.

Please do not mistake this praise with a claim that this work contains all the answers you need to deliver improved performance within your organization. In fact, after reading this book, you may come to realize that you are much further away from reaching your performance goals, even after years of a proactive, predictive, reliability based effort. Do not despair, just sit quietly and let this work open your eyes to why even the best ideas are subject to failure, and how sometimes the simplest solutions are discovered and implemented not at the top, but by the people closest to the problems.

I think that everyone who reads this book will recognize something about themselves and their organization in the pages that follow. My hope is that the recognition will allow the book to deliver an approach that increases respect for all of the people who make up an organization and who are vital in fulfilling the mission and vision that is the aim of the system being worked in. We all want to be Hero's.

Furthermore, I anticipate the other realization that will come from this work is that a great starting point for everyone is defect elimination. Performance improvements can make quantum leaps when defects are removed from the system. Without spoiling the ending, it turns out that people have a natural tendency to reduce defects when empowered to do so.

We are very fortunate to have a guide like Winston Ledet, who will continue to discover and search out new sources of wisdom, combine them with his own deep experience and knowledge and then shine a light that creates a path for us to follow.

Read this important book then lend the dog-eared copy to your plant manager.

Terrence O'Hanlon, CMRP,
CEO/Publisher
terrence@reliabilityweb.com

Disclaimer

Although this book is a work of fiction, it is based entirely on facts gathered from a number of sites and integrated into the fictional plant depicted in this story. The Lima Refinery, one of the plants studied, stands today as a testament to the hard work, perseverance, and dedication of its employees in the face of many obstacles and challenges. Because the Lima Refinery experienced a wildly successful Heroic Change Journey, Winston Ledet, with the help of many others, has spent years gathering the details and documenting each stage of the journey using that information to create a computer model to better understand and articulate the journey. This model has been used to help guide corporations in their own Heroic Change Journey to the improved Precision Domain with the help of a Dynamic Benchmarking and guidance process.

Inspirational Quote

The Chambered Nautilus

Year after year beheld the silent toil
That spread his lustrous coil;
Still, as the spiral grew,
He left the past year's dwelling for the new,
Stole with soft step its shining archway through,
Built up its idle door,
Stretched in his last-found home, and knew the old no more.

Build thee more stately mansions, O my soul,
As the swift seasons roll!
Leave thy low-vaulted past!
Let each new temple, nobler than the last,
Shut thee from heaven with a dome more vast,
Till thou at length art free,
Leaving thine outgrown shell by life's unresting sea!

-Oliver Wendell Holmes

Cast of Characters

James Emery	Plant Manager, Modern Products Manufacturing or MPM Atlanta
Carol Emery	James' wife
Marshall Jennings	James' boss, MPM corporate office
Don & Olivia Clark	Family friends of James & Carol
Lorraine Luby	James' assistant, MPM Atlanta
Vance Sullivan	James' Maintenance Manager, MPM Atlanta
Buzz McKenna	James' Operations Manager, MPM Atlanta
Frank Godfrey	Injured worker, MPM Atlanta
Todd Oldham	Most seriously injured worker, MPM Atlanta
Robert Monroe	Consultant, Maintenance and Reliability Systems or MRS
Reese Barnaby	Operations Shift Supervisor at the Extrusion line, MPM Atlanta
Chance Brooks	James' old boss, MPM corporate office
Mark Sterman	Renowned professor in the field of System Dynamics
Joe Miller	Maintenance Supervisor, MPM Atlanta
Steve Sarkey	Maintenance Supervisor, MPM Atlanta
Cindy	Network Engineer, MPM Atlanta
Susan Emery	James' daughter
Tommy Emery	James' son
Miss Ellen	Girl Scout Leader
Janet Stevens	VP of sales for James' division
Wayne Darby	Plant Comptroller, MPM Atlanta
Brooke	Susie's Girl Scout friend
Brian Evans	Operations Supervisor, MPM Atlanta
Chuck	A seasoned operator, MPM Atlanta
Billy Heard	Plant Manager, MPM Houston
Cheryl Demry	Plant Manager, MPM Philadelphia
Drew Weaver	Plant Manager, MPM Saint Louis
Louis Landry	Plant Manager, MPM Lake Charles
Sean Rayburn	Operations Manager, MPM Houston
Rico Martinez	Engineering Manager, MPM Houston

Table of Contents

Grateful Acknowledgements ... xi
Forward ... xiii
Disclaimer ... xvii
Inspirational Quote ... xix
Cast of Characters ... xxi

Chapter 1: A Reactive Leader ... 1
Chapter 2: The Call for Change ... 9
Chapter 3: An Action Plan ... 13
Chapter 4: A Gathering of Allies ... 29
Chapter 5: A Dismal Success ... 41
Chapter 6: A Long Lonely Road of Trials ... 69
Chapter 7: Who's in Control? ... 85
Chapter 8: Putting the Pieces Together ... 91
Chapter 9: Engaging the Organization ... 105
Chapter 10: The Less Direct Route ... 119
Chapter 11: Walking in the World of the Precision Domain ... 127
Chapter 12: A New Challenge ... 139
Chapter 13: In Which The Truth Is Revealed ... 151
Epilogue ... 155
About the Authors ... 159

A Reactive Leader

James Emery ran out the front door of his home on an unusually warm October day with an apple stuck in his mouth, frantically trying to shove papers in his briefcase and unlock his car door at the same time. He ducked his head as he folded himself into the car, and slouched down a bit so his head wouldn't hit the ceiling. His 6' 3" frame didn't fit well in compact cars, but he didn't have the time, or money, to upgrade to a bigger one. His day had begun at the crack of dawn, as they had every morning since he had taken over as plant manager at the Atlanta facility for Modern Products Manufacturing. He had been in the shower when the first calls started coming in, and had ended up standing in the bathroom in nothing but a towel, trying to solve problems over the phone. He deposited his apple on the console and looked at his hair in the mirror as he inserted his keys into the ignition. His hair had dried before he could blow it dry with some styling gel, leaving him with a bristly look. He sighed out loud as he noticed the slight graying that had recently appeared at the temples of his dark brown hair. His wife, Carol, claimed to like the look, saying it made him look distinguished. James would call it the effects of aging, aging due to the stress of his new job.

James backed his car out of the driveway and maneuvered into traffic as his thoughts turned to work. He had been in his new job for six months, and as he made the thirty minute drive in to work, he mentally ticked through the checklist of what he wanted to accomplish in the first year:

1. Get the plant to at least 85% of its rated capacity. Demand was strong in their industry and every unit produced increased their profitability.
2. Achieve 100% on-time and on-schedule deliveries to customers.
3. Reduce operating expenses by 10%. Corporate was constantly pushing this metric so he needed to show progress.
4. Get to a world class safety performance metric of less than 0.5 OSHA recordables per two hundred thousand man hours.
5. Become the choice within the company for new capital investment.

There was going to be expansion in the company, and James knew that a site with new investments would attract talent and generate excitement. To accomplish this, they would need to deliver on his first four goals and show they had the capacity to take on more. He had told the staff that these were his top five priorities only a few months ago, and yet, he had to admit he had made almost no progress on any of them. The day-to-day priorities of running the plant, along with the unexpected events that always seemed to pop up, had a way of crowding out his top five.

As he came up to the next red light, James took a bite of his apple then reached over to pull out his calendar, flipping the book open to check his schedule. He groaned out loud when he saw that meetings filled his entire day. So much for the top five today, James thought. He would be lucky to have the time to check and answer e-mails, plus handle anything else that could, and probably would, come up at the last minute. Realizing it was going to be another long day, he tossed his calendar onto the passenger seat in frustration. At least, he was in a good paying job with excellent benefits, and the company was world-renowned. He had faith that because he was working for such a good company, everything would eventually work itself out. Things would settle down, and his position as plant manager would be a nice, safe, respectable position. The company would stand behind him and support him, and when it did, he told himself, he would be a lot more comfortable and have the time to drive his top five.

After reaching the plant, he started toward his office, but never made it, as one of his leaders chased him down in the hall to request a "quick chat". By ten o'clock, he still hadn't made it to his office, and was still trying to put out fires from incidents that had happened overnight.

James finally made it to his office by ten-thirty and plopped down in his chair to review his e-mails before the next round of meetings. After having only enough time to go through the most urgent messages, he realized that he now had three meetings scheduled for eleven o'clock. He muttered under his breath about the craziness of his job, as he noticed an e-mail from Corporate. Marshall Jennings, his boss, wanted to know how the site ran yesterday and last night, prior to his nine o'clock meeting. "A little late for that now", James said out loud, looking at his watch and seeing it was almost eleven o'clock. He sighed, knowing that Corporate wanted more and more information - not just the numbers. The craze of the month among managers at Corporate was a book about getting to the bottom of things by asking five whys. Lately, every request for data was followed by a barrage of "whys". He also wondered why they never asked the "five whys" when things ran well, not that it happened very often anyway. James sighed.

The intercom on his desk buzzed as the annoyingly chipper voice of his very capable assistant, Lorraine Luby, announced another call. "Mr.

Emery, your wife is on line two for you."

James pushed back his chair in frustration, knowing he needed to deal with all of his scheduling glitches ASAP. "Thanks, Lorraine. Go ahead and put her through." He picked up the phone on the first ring. "James here," he said distractedly.

"Hey, Honey!" his wife's cheerful voice broke through the fog in his mind. "Just calling to see what time you're going to be home for dinner tonight because I've invited the Clarks over. They should arrive around six-thirty."

James clenched his teeth at the idea of dining with Don and Olivia Clark tonight. They never had anything more interesting to talk about than his golf game and her tennis lessons. It was all so nauseating. "Uh, I'm not sure. I'll try to be home by seven," James said, not feeling very optimistic about the time.

"Seven o'clock? James, can't you make it earlier than that?" Carol asked.

James ran a hand through his hair in frustration, feeling cornered. "I'll try Carol, but no guarantees."

Carol sighed heavily and replied, "Well, all right, I guess, but don't be later than that, okay?"

Starting to feel annoyed, he snapped back, "I said I'd try, Carol!" There was a long pause, and James could picture the hurt expression on his wife's face. "I'm sorry for snapping. It's just been a bad day," James relented.

"It's okay, Hon. I'll see you at home tonight for dinner. Bye," Carol replied, with a hurt sound in her voice.

James said goodbye and hung up the phone in frustration. His wife certainly did not deserve his short temper. The thought of the Clarks just really put him in a bad mood. If he was being honest with himself, maybe the problem was that he was a bit jealous. He could not remember the last time his golf clubs had come out of the garage. To hear Don constantly talking about his golf adventures made him jealous, James realized. This job is killing me, he thought to himself.

At one of his many meetings later that day, he listened to the latest urgent issues. As his subordinates vied for attention, and pointed out the problems with doing just about anything other than further study, he tuned them out for a moment.

He thought back and asked himself, "Didn't I handle these kinds of problems on my own, two promotions ago?" It would be nice if they'd make some decisions on their own, he thought, but they don't seem to have the time, interest, or confidence required to make decisions before urgent matters became yet another crisis. It was all a vicious, never-ending cycle. He noticed that everyone was looking at him, waiting for his decision, so he gave one without really taking the time to consider it.

At the end of the meeting, James barked out a few commands. He liked the feeling of control. In his position as plant manager, he had a lot more authority than he was used to as operations manager. It was a bit disconcerting that all of the decisions, and actions, had to be initiated by him, but if he didn't take control and force the issue, nothing was going to get done. Finally, people took their marching orders, and the meeting was adjourned so they could all get on with their day.

Close to the end of the day, James had settled into his routine paperwork when he heard the emergency siren go off. He grabbed his hard hat and hurried out of his office. As he rushed by his assistant's desk, he yelled over his shoulder, "Hey, Lorraine, find Vance, and find out what's going on." He glanced down at his phone, noticing a new message had come in, "Fire on the Forming Line". He proceeded to the area at a brisk pace thinking about the potential damage and the re-start procedures. He would have to cancel his last meeting of the day to oversee the start-up and ensure that it went smoothly. He made a mental note to send his assistant a message to cancel that meeting.

As he approached the forming line, he initially felt a sense of relief, followed quickly by a surge of panic. The relief came from seeing that the fire was small, well contained, and not impacting any of the major equipment. The panic came when he realized that it had taken him over five minutes to walk the distance from his office, and yet no one had begun fighting the fire. He knew that in a chemical plant, the situation could get out of control quickly. That's why they had their own fire fighting equipment and trained personnel to act as first responders. But where were they, he wondered in frustration. They had drilled and drilled on these types of scenarios. With a fire this size, they should already be here and have it under control. James, biting back a curse, walked up to a group that was clearly coordinating the non-response effort.

"Where the hell is the truck?" James bit out, trying to control his anger. "This damn thing is going to get out of control if we don't get on it!"

One of the area supervisors spoke up after a moment of hesitation and some nervous foot shuffling. "Well, when they went to roll the truck, they had engine problems and couldn't get it to start. They're going to have to tow it out here."

James looked at them incredulously, "Do you mean to tell me that we can't respond to this failure because those incompetents can't keep a truck running? What chance do we have?"

The fire truck, in tow chains, pulled up just as James finished his sentence and the volunteer crew scrambled out. This was James' worst nightmare. He could feel his blood pumping and his heart racing. He had to take a deep breath to calm himself as the crew, who were obviously frustrated, did their work.

James decided they were very efficient when, within ten minutes, they had the fire out with no material damage to the area. James, feeling immensely relieved, made a point of thanking the tow truck driver for being available and ready so quickly.

James hung around for another hour and a half. He felt compelled to make sure operations resumed normally. He took personal control of the situation and made sure that everything came back on line as quickly as possible.

As he started walking back to his office, James groaned out loud remembering that he had never found the time to send the message to Lorraine about canceling that last meeting of the day. "Damn!" he said, as he pulled out his phone and angrily punched in her number.

"Well, you missed your last meeting," Lorraine advised in a droll voice, skipping her usual chirpy greeting.

Lorraine had been James' assistant for six months now and he'd come to depend on her a great deal. She was in her mid-thirties with a no-nonsense look, a no-nonsense attitude and a wickedly dry sense of humor. She didn't take crap from anyone, and the fact that she called things as she saw them was invaluable to James. Her old fashioned attitude and formal ways, along with the fact that she meticulously observed the social proprieties while remaining somewhat aloof, often put people off, but not him. They worked well together, and James understood and respected her a great deal. There just wasn't much that got past Lorraine, and he benefited from her observations and strict work ethic.

"Your meeting was with quality control at Sterling Composites," Lorraine continued, "our number two customer you might remember."

James ran a hand through his hair and rolled his eyes at Lorraine's sarcasm, which he usually found amusing, but was not in the mood for at the moment, "Yeah, yeah, what'd they say?"

"I tap danced around and said you were dealing with an emergency, but he still seemed pretty ticked off. Sorry, it was the best I could do. He said he'd call you later."

James thanked Lorraine and hung up feeling worse.

As the afternoon turned into evening, his day did not improve. The quality control manager at Sterling had called around five o'clock and berated James for the constant quality issues that his company was experiencing with the products that James was sending them. He threatened that if things did not turn around quickly, his recommendation to the procurement managers would be to change sources for their material. James assured him that he would get to the bottom of the problem and arranged a new meeting.

James looked at his watch, realizing it was almost five-thirty and he still needed to attend to the quality issues before he could even think about wrapping it up for the day. His first stop was the mixing line. Given the customer's issues, James was fairly sure that the problem was in the mixing operation. He called in the area supervisors and manager and read them the riot act. He assured all of them that they would be replaced if they couldn't figure out how to get the job done right. He told them he wanted an answer on his desk in the morning. He left the meeting feeling that he had lit a fire under the team, but before he went back to his office he wanted to follow up on one more hunch with regard to Sterling Composites' quality problem.

Darkness was falling outside as James found himself at the top of a ladder that ascended a tank in the tank farm adjacent to the mixing line, where the raw materials were held in large reservoirs waiting to be mixed in a reactor to make the end product. He was holding a sample kit used to check the properties of the tank contents when he felt the hairs on the back of his neck stand up. He turned to look over his shoulder and saw two of his more experienced operators approaching. They were obviously surprised to see a shadowy figure up on the ladder, if their gaping mouths were any indication. They knew no one else was supposed to be in the area at this time of the day, and as they realized that the figure was their plant manager, their expressions turned from confrontational to perplexed.

"James...is there something that we can help you with?" one of the operators asked uncertainly.

James mentally cringed. He knew he shouldn't be up here, it simply was not his job, but he couldn't seem to help himself. "No, no, just following up on a hunch regarding quality problems in mixing," James responded sheepishly.

"Hmm," the operator replied, "My supervisor just sent me out here to collect samples. I guess there's no need for that now?" he asked hesitantly.

"No, I think that I've got it under control. It's pretty clear that we have a problem with the previous step, and the purity of one of the inbound components," James commented, as he gathered up his things and began to climb back down the ladder. He thanked the operators as he began to walk off in the direction of his office.

"Sure. Okay, well we'll see you later, James," one of the operators called after him.

The tank farm was much quieter than the rest of the plant, and James could just make out the conversation between the two of them as he rounded the corner out of sight.

"When he's out here doing our job, who's up there doing the plant manager's job?"

James almost laughed out loud at the comment, and he would have been especially amused had he been able to see the dumbfounded expressions on their faces, as they looked at each other and shrugged, then turned to leave the area.

If James was being honest, they had a point. He needed to be able to trust his employees to do their jobs, but his overwhelming sense of responsibility was making it hard to give up that control. He thought of the recent fire and resolved to do whatever it took to run a safer plant.

It was seven o'clock before he finally escaped the plant, and as he drove home, exhausted, he started to wonder why he could not seem to get off this treadmill. Site profits were down, production was down, and equipment was failing left and right. Employees were uptight and disgruntled, and turnover was higher than it should be. There was no time for training, so management quickly rushed new employees through a cursory overview, leaving team leaders responsible for double-checking all front line employees' work. It always seemed to demand more speed than he could muster. He began to laugh out loud as he visualized himself as a donkey with a dangling carrot just out of reach.

As he drove up the driveway to his home, he saw that it was seven-thirty and the Clark's car was already in the driveway. He sighed knowing that he was late for dinner again. He desperately tried to shift gears from manager with heavy responsibilities to family man with equally heavy responsibilities. He knew his family wanted and deserved good quality time, but he did not have the energy to focus his attention on them. What could he do? He knew that he would be divorced before the year was out if he did not make time for his wife and family.

He parked the car in the driveway next to the Clark's car and got out, reaching back in for his briefcase. He had some reports he needed to read that night, and knew that bringing his work home would irritate Carol.

He sighed, realizing he would have to do it later, once the Clarks were gone, and everyone was asleep.

Later that night, after enduring the Clarks' company for the entire evening, James sat at his desk in the study, enjoying the absolute silence of the house. Everyone was asleep, and it was almost midnight. He had just finished reading the reports he had brought home, and although he was exhausted, he could not help but think about work. There was excitement in every day's work, and he was proud of his ability to make quick decisions on the many topics that he constantly had to react to.

However, the reports he was looking at did not paint a rosy picture. Production was well below capacity, and as he did the arithmetic in his head, the plant was leaving at least twenty million dollars on the table. All of the break-ins and emergencies that he had been handling so well were eating up valuable production capacity. Atlanta costs were much higher than peer plants in MPM and costs were nowhere near world class. He wondered how he could be expected to do all of the work today, plus additional work to get production up and costs lowered. Frankly, it seemed like a trade-off between cost and production, and he often felt like telling Corporate they had to pick one or the other. They simply couldn't have both.

James felt that the ultimate answer was investment in the plant, but there was not much chance of that in the short term. Return on invested capital was the main measure used to make investment decisions. That measure also lagged behind his peers and industry benchmarks he'd seen. He found it all a little depressing and overwhelming.

Oh well, he thought, at least he had safety. He was among the leaders in the company, and not bad against the industry benchmarks. The numbers looked bad because of all the accidents that had happened before James had taken over. There had been no accidents in the six months of his tenure as plant manager. He felt lucky to at least have that to hang his hat on. There had been a string of near-misses at the plant, but none had resulted in injury, at least that was one thing he didn't have to worry about.

The trivial doubts always lingered in the back of his mind. He worried a great deal and knew he needed to make some changes, but was not sure how to go about it. He had been in the position for only a few months, and still felt that he was on trial with Corporate. He never had time to think twice about anything when at work. At night, when his mind could relax, his thoughts would inevitably turn to work. He worried about keeping up with the pace and about doing a good job. He worried about a lot of things. He let out a big sigh, realizing that he needed a game plan.

THE CALL FOR CHANGE

The next day, James woke up thirty minutes earlier than normal in hopes of getting into the office before the urgent calls started up. Unfortunately, the phone started ringing while he was still getting dressed.

It seemed that there had been two production disruptions overnight. Corporate wanted a report and, more importantly, they were going to be short for one of their key deliveries. He spent fifteen minutes choosing which customer to short, and another half hour getting yelled at by that customer for failing to meet the scheduled production and balling up the customer's production process.

He spent so much time on the phone at home, that now he was running late again, and he knew he had an eight o'clock meeting. He jumped in the car as Carol chased after him, trying to hand him a banana because he had skipped breakfast again. He rolled down the window to take the banana and smiled gratefully at his wife, admiring the fact that she was still a good looking woman, even after two kids. She always looked polished, even first thing in the morning. She was also a good wife, a loving mother, and a more than capable homemaker, which he appreciated because he sure hadn't been any help on the home front lately with the time he spent at the plant. He blew her a kiss, and gave her a wink and a smile, as he pulled out of the driveway, but the smile dropped from his face the minute he pulled away. He headed out of his neighborhood towards the office with a sick feeling in the pit of his stomach.

"What more could go wrong today?" he asked out loud.

James hadn't even taken a sip of his coffee before Lorraine walked in his office getting straight to the point with bad news in the form of the plant's latest routine scorecard results.

Key Performance Indicator	Description	Atlanta Plant Current Year Forecast	Best in Class
Atlanta Scorecard 1 - October 2nd			
Maintenance as a % of Replacement Value	Maintenance cost, excluding capital compared to the estimated capital cost to replace the plant equipment	3.4%	2%
Overtime %	Percent of overtime for hourly workers	25%	<5%
Waste cost as a percent of raw materials cost	The cost of all scrap and defective output compared to total input	2.1%	0.2%
Raw material cost per ton of output	Applied only to plants making similar outputs	$18.74	$20
Labor cost per ton of output	Applied only to plants making similar outputs	$12.14	$7.30
Consumables, parts and outside repairs cost per ton		$5.32	$2.50
Energy costs per ton		$7.64	$7.25
% Planned Maintenance Work	% of work that is planned and scheduled at least 1 week in advance	0%	95%
Production % of Max	Maximum production the plant can operate at	81%	98%
Earnings	Last 12 months earnings in millions of dollars	$4.1 million (loss)	$40 million (profit)
Recordable injuries/ 200K man hours		2.45	<0.50

The numbers were dismal, and James couldn't stop worrying about them as he distractedly attended a meeting later that morning. He listened with half an ear while working the score card numbers in his head, thinking his day couldn't possibly get much worse. Unfortunately, it got worse than James could have ever imagined.

He was still in his ten o'clock meeting when Lorraine rang in to the conference room to let him know that there had been an accident with one of the compressors. He quickly called the meeting to an end and headed down to the compressor building. When he entered the area, he was surprised to see two teams of paramedics. Each team was apparently working on someone. James' heart lurched as he strained to see around the gathered crowd.

His maintenance manager, Vance Sullivan, came over and stood at his shoulder. After a long silence, he finally offered an explanation, "The compressor just flew apart, and some of the blades flew out, hitting a couple of the guys."

James glanced over at one of the men who was lying on the floor and visibly blanched when he saw a pool of blood on the floor. "How many people were injured?" James asked.

"We really lucked out. Five minutes before it blew, we had thirty guys in the area. Thankfully, the majority of them had just left for a break. Frank Godfrey and Todd Oldham were the only two hit by blade debris. I don't know how serious it is, but I think they'll be fine."

James' brows knitted together in concern as the men were loaded onto stretchers and carried out. He felt a bit nauseous as the crowd cleared and he saw the after-effects of the accident. His thoughts turned to another time and place he couldn't bear to remember.

He broke into a cold sweat and his heartbeat escalated as he thought of the day that had changed the way he viewed life and death forever. He'd been a high school kid, working one summer with his best friend, Ben, in a furniture making company. James had been telling one of his famous jokes, and just as he had delivered the punch line, Ben was pushing a board through a lathe. Ben had laughed out loud, taking his eyes off of what he was doing for a split second, but that split second was all it took. Ben's hand had been caught by the lathe and severed.

The memory of that day had always haunted James. Although Ben later recovered, minus the hand that could not be reattached, James had always felt an overwhelming sense of guilt that had never abated, even though his good-natured friend held no hard feelings and did not blame him. But James had always blamed himself. He shook his head to clear the images of that ugly day and wiped the sweat from his brow. He headed to the bathroom to splash some cold water on his face. This was going to be a long day.

James later learned that Frank had a broken arm, some lacerations to his head, and a major concussion, which would keep him in the hospital overnight for observation. Todd's condition was a bit worse, with broken ribs, cuts, and lacerations to the upper part of his body, including an eye injury that could cost him his sight.

James sat in his office that afternoon with his head in his hands, feeling mentally and physically exhausted. He had spent the day trying to mitigate the damage from the accident, and worrying about Frank and Todd. He was thankful that more people were not injured. At the same time, he felt sick at heart to know that Frank and Todd sustained injuries on his watch.

He knew that a number of people probably contributed to the cause of the accident. If he were being honest with himself, he guessed there were things he could have done himself to prevent it. Over the last couple of months, he'd specifically brought up safety with Vance and a few other managers and not been very reassured. He'd let it slide, and in hindsight, he should have been more persistent and pressed for more specific answers to his questions with regard to safety.

The thought was sobering. "I totally failed these guys!" he said under his breath. He hated to face the facts, but there had been numerous signs over the past few weeks that safety was becoming more and more lax. He should have addressed it. He should have done something, but he hadn't. He'd let it go simply because he didn't want to make waves. It was easier. He could get out of the office earlier each night if he wasn't stirring the pot. He'd been trying to appease his wife, and in the process, he'd jeopardized the safety of his employees.

He thought, *maybe I'm not ready for this job, and maybe, with a stronger leader and a better manager, those guys wouldn't have been hurt.* But he quickly wiped that train of thought from his mind. He thought about Frank and Todd and their families, and right then made a vow as he clenched his fists. He needed to make some drastic changes around here. He needed to ensure that no other accidents happened at his site, if it was the last thing he did. It was going to mean a lot less time at home and, of course, the kind of changes he had in mind could not be accomplished by him alone. He was going to need some allies.

AN ACTION PLAN

After a sleepless night, James drove to work with a new sense of purpose. A root cause review meeting of the incident was planned first thing in the morning. They now had a good understanding of why the accident had occurred. Vance, as the maintenance manager, had been tasked with creating an initial assessment. He had reported that the over speed trip mechanism had not been tested for almost five years. It did not trip the compressor when the throttle valve failed in the open position, making the compressor go faster and faster. It finally flew apart, resulting in a catastrophic event. The throttle valve had been sticking for weeks, but the operators had learned how to baby it and keep it from failing. Because of another incident earlier in the day, none of the experienced operators were there for start-up and a relatively new and inexperienced operator did not know that special start-up procedures were needed. Frankly, they were just lucky that more workers had not been injured or even killed.

After the review meeting, James called in his entire group of managers and leaders for a meeting. He opened the meeting with his belief about the accident and the last few months of underperformance, "I'm convinced that the same issues that led to yesterday's accident are creating our production issues as well. If we can get this place under better control, we can eliminate both problems."

Everyone nodded in agreement. "We do not have proper maintenance going on in the plant!" James declared. "As a result, there is far too much surprise work and too many disruptions."

James took a long pause to look at each one of his managers, to emphasize the importance of his next statement, "As we learned yesterday, when it all goes wrong, people get hurt." James then stated, softly but firmly, noticing how everyone leaned in to hear, "That is simply unacceptable."

"Now, wait a minute!" Vance spoke up, clearly insulted as he was in charge of maintenance. "I'll grant you that the trip indicator was faulty and hadn't been checked, but no one from operations ever submitted a work order for it and those 'donut eaters' never told us about the problems with the throttle valve."

James cringed at the insult directed at his operations manager. "Donut eater" was Vance's favorite of many insults he often hurled at the operations team. Vance looked like your typical engineer, with clothes that never fit quite right and an odd precision to everything he did. He was tall, lanky, and had stringy brown hair. James believed that he was a very effective maintenance manager because he knew the equipment exceptionally well and was smart as a whip. He could be counted on to keep things running at the plant, but he could never get along with anyone in operations, and he was always very defensive.

As expected, Buzz McKenna, the operations manager, sat bolt upright in his seat, bristling at the insult. Buzz was a middle-aged, ex-Marine still sporting a precision military flat top. He believed in the chain of command, and even at his age, could probably still take anyone at the plant, or he certainly acted like he could. Twenty years later, he no longer had the body of a Marine, with a fairly pronounced beer belly, but he certainly had the size and the attitude. He often surprised James in that he was much more trusting of the front-line than James was comfortable with. He would often say that a squad was only as strong as its weakest member, which always left James hoping that it wasn't true.

"I didn't realize it was our job to write your standing preventative maintenance work orders now," Buzz shot back sarcastically.

While the two were friends outside of the plant, and seemed to like each other personally, they were constantly at each other at work blaming the other's department for their problems.

James interrupted before their argument could get out of hand, "I am not trying to assess blame here. I'm simply pointing out the facts. We don't have adequate controls in place, and we're reacting to far too many incidents. I believe we need to tackle this together as a team." When no one offered up further arguments, James continued, "Vance and Buzz, I want you two to pull together a team to pursue this, and I want you both to help lead it. I'll personally be involved to make sure everyone understands that this is my top priority."

They each offered up a list of names for the team. As they completed the list, James had a nagging thought that these were the same people who were put up for every special team. He supposed that made sense since they were among the most motivated and experienced people at the plant. He conceded that it was due to their knowledge and leadership ability, and it was best to tap into those strengths. He just wondered what some new blood might be able to do. When the list was completed, James looked at his watch and knew it was time to wrap up the meeting.

"We need to clearly communicate as a team what the next steps are going to be and how we are going to prevent future incidents. I'm counting on each of you to communicate to your teams and get the message out.

First, I want everyone in the plant to understand the root causes of this failure. Second, I want each operations team to list the components that haven't been inspected in their area for over a year. I want those lists to Vance by the end of the day tomorrow. If that one compressor's over speed trip mechanism had not been tested for almost five years, I want to know what other problems could be lurking. Third, I want all irregular operations, like the stuck valve on the compressor, documented, and an assessment done and signed off on by the operations supervisor in the area, as to whether or not the irregular operation is safe. Fourth, for any irregular operations that we deem safe, I want to have a training session created for all workers in the area to go through."

James paused a moment to let them finish their writing. When everyone was clearly done writing, and he had all of their attention, he asked, "Are those four steps clear?" When everyone nodded, James added, "Any issue with communicating that to your teams today?" Everyone shook their heads. Now we'll see some action, thought James. "Great! Let's get back to work." Everyone stood up and shuffled out of the conference room.

James later received a sobering call from Human Resources letting him know that Todd had lost the sight in his injured eye, putting a huge weight on James' shoulders. Just the thought of someone losing his sight because of his failure as a plant manager was more than James could bear. The HR manager said that Todd was very self-conscious about the injury and did not want the news spread widely. She told James that she was only informing him. After he'd hung up with HR, he sat in his office thinking. "This stops here," he muttered out loud to himself.

A minute later, the phone rang. James could see from the caller id that it was Marshall Jennings, his boss from Corporate. Marshall was like a bull dog. He was in his late forties, and completely focused on achieving results. He was unmarried and didn't seem to have a social life of any kind, if the amount of time he spent working was any indication. He never even used his vacation time. He also never stopped pushing for results.

They had talked off and on over the past twenty-four hours regarding the accident and steps to prevent its re-occurrence. Earlier that morning, he and Jennings had crafted the four point plan that James had used to close the staff meeting.

As they were pulling the plan together, Jennings had reiterated, "The only way to get this kind of change done is to engage your entire formal organizational structure. It is time to lay down the law."

James picked up the phone, and before he could say hello, Jennings, ignoring the usual salutations, got to the business at hand. "James, I have my flight booked," Jennings announced. "I'll be there by ten o'clock tomorrow morning and I'll have Robert Monroe from MRS with me".

James learned that Corporate had engaged Maintenance and Reliability Systems (MRS). They were widely known as the best at installing planned maintenance systems and approaches. His guess was that the accident had nominated him to be the guinea pig. Oh well, this might be exactly what they needed right now.

James took some time, right after lunch, to check in with the plant workers and get a feel for how they were doing after the accident, and to see if the message from this morning was starting to make the rounds. He stopped in at the Extrusion line and saw an old friend, Reese Barnaby, who was the shift supervisor. He and Reese went way back, and had worked together years ago.

Today, Reese didn't look so happy. James stopped and gave Reese a pat on the back. "Well, how is the team holding together?" James asked.

"Ok, I guess," replied Reese, distractedly. "Everyone feels terrible about Todd's eye. It makes you think, I guess."

James nodded his agreement, not knowing exactly how much Reese knew about Todd's injury. James opted not to go into detail with Reese. The HR manager had assured him that she would not mention the extent of the injuries to anyone else, so if Reese did know the full extent of the injury, James was shocked at how fast the news had traveled.

"And if that weren't enough, Buzz has got us doing a bunch of busy work!" Reese interjected.

That got James' attention. He had been afraid his four point plan would be ignored.

Reese continued, "Buzz has us cataloging all sensors, and logging their readings for the last month. He wants it by end of day for Vance. Then he asked for a full operations guide for the line. Hell, I just gave him that a month ago. I guess I'll just put a new cover on it and give it to him again."

James stood there, slack jawed. He recognized the busy work. It was a Frankenstein version of his four point plan. Buzz, his ex-Marine, had butchered it. James asked, "Reese, did Buzz cover with your team the root cause of yesterday's accident?"

"No," Reese said, looking confused. "Buzz gave me the rundown this morning, but we don't have any compressors on this line, so my guys don't give a crap about that gibberish."

James nodded slowly, clenching his teeth, not sure who he should be more upset with. "Well, Reese, I asked that everyone hear the root causes, and I would like you to deliver the message to your team. As for the busy work, I think Buzz and I had a miscommunication, and I'll straighten that out. Why don't you hold off on his request until I have a chance to talk with him."

Reese seemed a little taken aback. "Oh, okay James. I'll get right on it," he said, in a tone that clearly indicated he had thought he was having an informal conversation with an old friend, and now realized he was having a work conversation with his boss.

James walked away fuming. How could word of Todd's injury travel so quickly and yet his four point plan get so butchered? He was especially annoyed because it was all supposed to be kept quiet. He was going to see Buzz immediately. As usual though, he was interrupted on his walk to Buzz's office, this time by Steve Sarkey, one of his maintenance supervisors.

Steve noticed him coming down the hall and stopped him, asking, "James, do you have a minute? Vance walked out of your staff meeting pretty fired up this morning. He asked us to pull all of the compressor failures for the last two years and document what percentage failed with irregular operations, and how many had unreported problems. James, you know our system. There is no way to get at that kind of data. The only way to do it is to interview the operators for each failure and get their opinion. We started to do that but they all say that Buzz has them doing a bunch of documentation work of their own, and they don't have time. Plus, Buzz got wind of what we're doing and told the operators not to cooperate because we were on a witch hunt to prove that operations is at fault. I'm kind of stuck between a rock and a hard place here."

James sighed, realizing things were spinning out of control. "I'm on my way to see Buzz now. I'll touch base with him and Vance, and we will get you some clear direction".

Steve clapped him on the back with a relieved smile, "Thanks, James, appreciate it."

James flashed a pained smile and continued his search for Buzz. He found him in his office, and was pleased to see Vance there as well. Good, he thought to himself, I can set them both straight.

Unfortunately, he'd walked into a heated argument. Because their voices were getting loud enough to carry, James glanced over his shoulder quickly to make sure nobody was looking, and quietly closed the door for more privacy. Since his entrance had gone unnoticed, James leaned against the closed door, crossed his arms in annoyance, and loudly cleared his throat for attention. When his presence had still gone unnoticed, James rolled his eyes, and before their bickering back and forth got further out of hand, interrupted, "I thought I was clear this morning on what needed to be done. Yet none of your people seem to have gotten the message."

Startled by the interruption, Buzz and Vance's argument came to a screeching halt in mid-sentence. They sheepishly looked at the floor as James continued, "Buzz, I need you to go back to the teams and deliver the message from this morning, and tell them precisely what I need. No embellishments or pet projects. Vance, I need your team focused on a preventative maintenance plan for all of the items that Buzz's team uncovers. Guys, we have to be a team on this. Jennings will be here tomorrow, and he is going to expect to see some progress." With that he opened the door and walked out of the office.

James worked in his office until late in the evening, trying to prepare for the next day. He knew he would be forced to make a lot of decisions about how to go forward. He thought about what he would like to see in a planned maintenance strategy. He would have to shift the balance of power from his operations manager to his maintenance manager to make sure all the new work took priority. That was going to be a big shift, and he was not sure how Buzz, being the operations manager, would take it. James resolved to have his detailed plan formulated by the end of the week so he could begin implementing it the following week.

Because James knew that Jennings' arrival would blow the whole day, he arrived at work before dawn in an attempt to get all of his administrative work and e-mails completed before Jennings and the consultant from MRS arrived.

At ten, Lorraine buzzed in on the intercom, "James, I see Mr. Jennings and Mr. Monroe down the hall. They're being mobbed by handshakes and brown-nosers right now, but they should make it to your office shortly."

James chuckled to himself as the intercom clicked off. No response was ever necessary with Lorraine, and she kept him laughing. He closed the file he was working on and quickly straightened his desk. By the time he stepped out of his office, his guests had just walked up. He greeted Jennings, and was introduced to Robert Monroe from MRS. Robert was short, overweight, and sported a full head of thick, startling white hair. He looked a bit like a round cotton ball, James thought to himself, as he reached out to shake his hand. James escorted them both to the large conference room where they exchanged small talk before getting down to business.

Robert took a sip of his coffee, put down the mug, and leaned back in his chair looking around the conference room. "You know, James, I've visited here before. Ten years ago, I think it was." James was startled when he realized that ten years ago would mean that he was here before MPM had acquired the plant. "What were you doing back then?" James asked.

"Same stuff," replied Robert, "we put in a planned maintenance system."

"Oh, was it scrapped mid-stream or something?" James asked with a look of surprise on his face.

"No, we finished on time and on budget," replied Robert, without a hint of how the plant could be so far from planned maintenance today.

He was hesitant to press him for further answers with Jennings in the room, so James made a mental note to ask more questions later, when he could get Robert alone. He really needed to understand what had happened ten years ago.

For the next three hours, which included a working lunch that Lorraine had ordered and brought in for them, James, Jennings, and Robert, sat and reviewed and plotted the essentials of putting in a planned system.

The rationale was compelling enough. Robert had tons of data showing how much less expensive, and more productive, plants were with these systems in place. Many of the best practices came out of Europe, and US companies like Alumax, which was a subsidiary of Alcoa. Maintenance costs could be 30% less, while uptime and capacity 10-15% more. Those would be huge numbers for his plant. Additionally, Robert painted a picture of life in a planned mode and it sounded great. No more calls in the middle of the night, fewer accidents, less missed orders. It sounded so good in fact, James was almost drooling. It sounded just like what James needed.

However, the implementation sounded a little daunting. The three of them based the plan for the Atlanta Plant on the generic model that Robert presented at the beginning of the meeting. Robert made the whole thing sound like a military operation. This appealed to James in his current situation. He needed some discipline, some adherence to standards, and as Jennings stated earlier he needed to "lay down the law."

First, the plant would have to put together a preventive maintenance (PM) program. There would be a sub-team to handle that. The idea was to identify all of the wear parts in the plant and create a cycle for checking and replacing them, the same idea as a 10,000 mile check up for a car. The steps James had put in place the previous day would help get the target list of machines and components identified, and Robert had some great benchmark data to give the sub-team on other places to look. The goal was to have this preventive piece up and running in three weeks.

Second, they would put in place a predictive maintenance (PdM) program. The sub-team for this project would focus on detecting problems through monitoring and inspection. They would then write work orders based on inspections, and maintenance would repair the issue before there was a failure. This would also require planners to set up the work plan, kit the parts for the jobs, and create a scheduling function in operations to determine the best time to take the equipment out for service. This phase would take longer, but the plan was to have it up in eight to twelve weeks.

Third, they would put a proactive maintenance program in place. MRS would deploy five trained facilitators to the plant to facilitate reliability centered maintenance (RCM) analysis on key equipment. RCM, Robert explained, was a comprehensive methodology for cataloging all of the ways a piece of equipment could fail and the potential effects of those failures. Once the failure modes and effects were identified, strategies would be developed to deal with each. Some minor or very uncommon failures might be allowed to happen reactively, but many would become either PM jobs or have a monitoring program set up. In some cases, if the design was found to be at fault, a capital project might be called for to upgrade the equipment.

In reality, this would feed the planned maintenance program with more work once it became mature. This sub-team would not start until after the PM program was fully in place and would take an additional five weeks to do the initial assessments.

Finally, there was the computerized maintenance management system (CMMS). The Atlanta plant was using a home grown system that did not really have the capability to accommodate any of the new programs, so while the three phases were initiated, MRS would work on replacing the CMMS. This part, in particular, made James nervous. He had been through many system conversions in his career, and he could not remember any of them going smoothly, but Robert insisted that it was critical to success.

Robert also suggested that they conduct a full plant assessment that included both a review of metrics and a survey of employee practices.

\multicolumn{4}{c}{**MRS Schematic of Planned Maintenance Initiative**}			
Item	**Description**	**Timing**	**Scheduled Completion**
Preventive Maintenance	Sub Team to identify all the wear parts in the plant and set up a cycle of replacing them	Goal is to have up and running in 3 weeks	Oct. 22nd
Predictive Maintenance	Sub Team focus on monitoring and inspection to repair before a failure	Goal is to have it in place in 8-12 weeks	Nov. 26th to Dec. 24th
Proactive Maintenance	Deploy 5 MRS facilitators to do RCM analysis	Goal is to have it done 5 weeks after PM program starts	Oct. 27th to Nov. 26th
Upgrade CMMS	MRS would work on replacing the existing CMMS	While the other programs are being initiated, MRS will start the conversion	By year end
Plant Assessment, including a review of metrics and a survey of employee practices	The metrics on the existing score card may need to be upgraded	We should review the score cards roughly every quarter	Ongoing

As 1:30 rolled around, they had the plan pretty well laid out, and were feeling pretty optimistic. They were taking a quick break to make call backs and use the restroom, when James caught Jennings in the break room alone. He used the opportunity to ask one of the questions that had been lingering in his mind as the plan was coming together.

"This plan is really taking shape, Jennings. I was wondering what kind of budget you had to put behind this. It just seems that all of these programs, at least in the beginning, are going to take some investment."

Jennings looked over his shoulder to see if they were alone before answering. "James, there is no extra budget for this effort. You have your operating budget. You have to make it fit within that. You saw the benchmark figures this morning – 30% cost savings. Surely 30% cost savings will fund the effort. Corporate of course is paying for the software. You'll just need to cover the costs from MRS."

"What?" exclaimed James, choking on the coffee he'd just sipped from his coffee mug. "You are not even covering the cost of the consultants? How much is that going to be?"

"Robert tells me it runs between half a million to a million dollars per plant," Jennings said matter-of-factly.

James' head was spinning. The plan that had seemed like his salvation while sitting in the conference room a few minutes ago, now felt like a noose around his neck.

Jennings, picking up on James' shock added, "James, look, this is still your plant, and it's your operating budget. I'm not going to tell you how to spend it, but come on, you can't have another accident like the one this week and don't forget… 30% savings." He patted him on the back and headed back to the conference room with his cup of coffee.

James looked down into his own cup of coffee and wondered what the job market looked like right now. He mentally shook off his doom and gloom thoughts and followed Jennings back into the conference room to wrap up their meeting.

After taking Jennings to the airport, and working with Robert to put the finishing touches on the plan, James turned it over to Lorraine to work up an electronic version to share with the team in the next day's staff meeting. Although he still had misgivings about the cost, James didn't see an alternative to launching the plan.

At the end of the day, James packed up his briefcase, checked his e-mails one last time, and headed out to the parking lot. He glanced at his watch as he was opening his car door and realized it was already seven-thirty. "Jeez!" he said out loud, knowing he'd missed dinner again. At least he could count on Carol to have left a plate warming for him on the stove, James thought, as he buckled up and pulled out of the parking lot.

That evening, James sat at the table eating his warmed up dinner while Carol sat with him sipping her tea. He recapped the day's events as she sat quietly listening, the concern on her face becoming more and more evident.

"I don't like it," she said. "If you're right, and all of these initiatives add so much cost in such a short time, how do you think Jennings and the others at Corporate will respond?"

"Let's just say it won't be pretty," James replied, as he pushed back his empty plate and sat back.

Carol sighed and asked, "Do you think that this could have a negative impact on your career?"

"Well," James said, pausing because he wasn't sure if he should worry her, "I got the distinct impression from Jennings today that things had to improve."

"Isn't there someone you could talk to about this? Someone you can trust and who would have your best interests at heart?" Carol asked.

James instantly thought of his old boss who was now working at Corporate, Chance Brooks. He knew Chance thought like he did. Chance had been his mentor and confidant from the very beginning of his career. He was a bit of a legend in the company. He ran the St. Louis plant in its heyday and had achieved the highest throughput at the lowest operating cost in history. It was such an unbelievable performance that, even now, a decade later, most of James' peers believed it was more urban legend than fact, even though the St. Louis plant had continued to be the top performing plant for more than a decade. Even though Chance was getting a little long in the tooth and was about to retire, he was still a genius, with an intuitive sense for how to run a plant and lead a team.

Unfortunately, it was difficult to learn intuition, but Chance had always attempted to impart his wisdom to others. There was still so much to learn from him, and James knew he would miss his expertise and "on-target" advice when he retired, but, until then, James knew he would be the ideal person to offer up a little advice.

"Uhm...," James replied, "maybe I should give Chance Brooks a call and see if he can give me some advice to get me out of this dilemma." He looked at Carol as she smiled back at him, nodding her head in agreement.

"That would be a great idea, James!"

James smiled back at his wife as a new idea came to mind. He stood to pick up his plate, "Actually, I think I have an idea." James headed to the kitchen with his plate, rinsing it off and putting it in the dishwasher, then headed to his office to make a call.

He picked up the phone to dial Chance's number at home. Chance picked up on the second ring. After exchanging pleasantries, and catching up on the comings and goings of their respective families, James shifted to the reason for his call. He explained the plant's performance issues, all of the reactive emergency work, the accident, and the planning meeting with MRS. James conveyed his reservations about the costs and the sheer magnitude of the undertaking without any corporate support.

Chance chuckled a bit before responding. "It's like a bad flash back. I remember in the 80's when I was working at the Madison plant, you know, the plant that was later sold? Well, we had a big corporate-wide push into planned maintenance. I had all of the same concerns that you have now, and I was the guinea pig."

"How did it turn out?" James asked, guessing part of the answer since the Madison plant had been performing at the norm for the company, which meant very limited planned work.

"Well, pretty good at first. We saw some results in the plant performance, and made a real impact on some stubborn defects. But, ultimately, we never saw the cost improvements that the benchmarks suggested. In fact, costs went up for a while. I always felt that if we could have stuck with it a bit longer, we might have turned the corner."

Not exactly the answer James had been looking for. However, one thing that Chance mentioned intrigued him, "You used the term defect,

Chance. That word has been rolling around in my head for the last three days since the accident. What do you mean by that?"

"Well, in my time as a plant manager, I came to regard defects as my real enemy. I always thought of them as the little imperfections that caused all of our problems and upsets. Some were big and some small, but when they lined up in just the right way…kaboom!!! A catastrophe would hit."

Interesting, thought James, as he jotted in his notebook: Defects — the source of our problems, but what causes them?

Chance interrupted his thoughts, "Maybe we can help each other out. The guys here at Corporate have asked that I put together a manual on manufacturing excellence and change for my swan song before retirement. You know me, always a better doer than explainer. Maybe we could work on it together and solve both of our problems."

James liked the idea very much. "It sounds great!" he replied. "I think I have your first topic," and he went on to explain the note that he had just written down in his notebook.

Chance replied, "That's a really interesting question that I am just starting to get some definition around. I have some budget money that I'm using to fund a research project, with a professor at MIT in Boston, to study that topic, among others, and create a simulation of a plant going through a transition in performance. I chose him because I've been reading some of the work by Peter Senge and the System Dynamics group at MIT. They have this notion that structure creates behavior, or that the way systems interconnect, and the decisions we make, cause the performance that we see.

"I can't shake the feeling that we keep seeing this movie in plant reliability over and over again. There's too much reactive work. We struggle to implement programs for improvement only to see the plants fall back into their old ways and old results. Since we see it again and again, in different plants in different locations with different leadership, it has to be more than just isolated circumstances. It has to be something more systemic.

"If it's okay with you, James, I'd love for Atlanta to be the site we model. I'd need to send a couple of folks down there for a week to interview people and collect some data. After that, it will only require some review sessions and follow up questions. I'll be their sounding board for the modeling effort."

James was unsure of the value but couldn't see how it would hurt anything, so he agreed to be the guinea pig, even though he wasn't quite sure what he was signing up for. The two spent another half-hour talking and plotting, and set up a time to talk again soon.

James walked into the plant the next day feeling hopeful again. The talk with Chance had made him feel better about the plan and the future. At least, given time, Chance thought that it could work.

That morning, in the conference room where they hatched the plan, Robert walked James' leadership team through it, step by step. Vance loved it. He was like a kid at Christmas getting all of the new toys he wanted. He had an "I told you so" look planted on his face that was unmistakable. The rest of the team members were harder to read. They certainly seemed to agree with parts, but some of the MRS steps seemed to puzzle them.

As Robert was wrapping up the CMMS computer system installation, James felt the same way he sensed most of his team felt, completely overwhelmed. But there was no time for that now. The lights clicked on in the conference room and James asked, "Well, what questions do you have?"

Buzz, the operations manager, went first, "Are we really going to tackle all of this without any additional resources and without any corporate funding?"

"Well, we will have the MRS people in here for the next six months, but, yes, this is funded from our own operating budget," James replied.

Buzz nodded slowly and his eyebrows rose in a way that confirmed comprehension but not necessarily approval.

There were a few more questions about specifics, and then the leadership team proceeded to make assignments for the sub-teams. With so many teams, they had to dig deeper into the pool of candidates than normal, but they identified the twenty-five people that would be on the teams. They set a kick-off date for each of the sub-teams and adjourned the meeting. James was pleased that the plan was set and about to get underway.

The professor and his research assistant arrived the following week from MIT. James chuckled under his breath when he saw the professor, complete with short beard and tweed jacket sporting patches on the elbows. He could have been sent down from central casting. Mark Sterman was a renowned professor in the field of System Dynamics and had created models for a host of industries.

They got down to business, and James marveled at how quickly Mark started into the tough questions. Mark wanted to understand what made equipment fail, how they decided what to work on, who made the decisions, what they did if resources were not available, how long it took to train a skilled mechanic and on and on.

Mark also took down the names of experts in the plant on topics that he thought were important, and probed James for relevant data sources to build the model from. All the while, the silent research assistant took notes. Mark ended the session by giving James a basic primer on System Dynamics.

"There are a couple of central tenants of System Dynamics that we believe govern the behavior of systems. The first is feedback. Feedback in a system occurs when there is action that creates an output and an observation, and that observation triggers other actions. Generally, we think of feedback in loops, or circles, that are self-reinforcing or self-balancing. For example, take your answer to my question about staffing and overtime." As he continued to explain, he walked over to James' whiteboard and started sketching out a diagram of what he was outlining. "You answered that a supervisor looks at the workload for the week, or day, and the estimated work hours. If the required hours are greater than the hours available, the supervisor first looks to see if any of the work can be moved to a later schedule."

With that comment, Mark closed the circle on the first loop explaining, "That is a balancing feedback loop with a goal seeking behavior. The company policy, to balance the workload using existing resources, is to drive overtime to zero. If work could not be deferred, some supervisors might shorten the time allowed per job to make it fit. The result you indicated was still overtime, but it was just unplanned. Alternatively, the supervisor could simply plan for the overtime. These are also balancing loops, but the goal of them is to drive the backlog of important jobs to zero, rather than eliminate overtime.

"When I asked how far you would allow overtime to go, you said that for a short spike, say a week, you could tolerate as much as 30%, if there were a real emergency, but that your metrics made it almost impossible to sustain anything above 10%." Mark drew in these balancing loops as well.

It was fascinating to James to see his policies articulated in this way. He was still not sure how it was going to help him at the plant, but it did point out with much greater clarity the policies that had become the 'rules of the game' of which he was no longer aware.

Mark continued, "The second type of feedback that we look for in a system is self-reinforcing feedback. A classic one in manufacturing is scale economics. As you know, there are a lot of fixed costs at a facility like this one. When you're able to run more production through the facility, you're able to spread those fixed costs across a greater volume. That, in turn, lowers your cost per unit, allowing you to go to the marketplace to attract more business, increasing your volume.

"When the self-reinforcing loop works in your favor, you tend to think of it as a virtuous cycle. When it is harming you, you tend to think of it as a vicious cycle. Self-reinforcing feedback is often where the leverage is in a system, and we look very carefully for it when we are modeling.

"The one other thing that we focus on when we model is time, and the effects of time. Generally, we find that even managers who make good decisions and are strong analytically do not deal well with time delays and the problems these delays create in systems. They often attribute the effects that are caused by time delays in their own system to outside forces."

Mark walked over to the white board and began writing, as he continued talking, "We ran into an example of this with a recent client, and you'll easily relate to this.

"They were growing, and needed to ramp up resources to deal with the growth. This would be similar to the growth in planned work that you described to me as part of your new plan. Just like here, this growth caused the manager to hire more resources, and these resources, like yours, needed specialized skills. To get these skills, the newbies had to work and learn from the old hands.

"The immediate impact was an unintended loss of productivity, and an even greater problem dealing with growth. The manager had not thought through the time delay of getting productive resources, and the feedback inherent in the systems, and therefore was surprised to see the performance get worse before it got better."

Interesting, James thought to himself. James' brows knitted together as he realized how uncertain their preparations were. Had they allowed for this dynamic in their plan? James' thoughts jumped from one question to the next in a blur of internal questions.

Mark put his marker away and brushed his hands together, satisfied his explanation was clear, and obviously making an impact, if James' look of concentration was any indication. Mark thanked James for his time, and left James to his musings as he exited the room to meet with the others they had set up interviews with.

Chapter 4

A GATHERING OF ALLIES

Two months after the accident, James found himself in his office going over some reports while he ate an early lunch.

As he absently stared at a column of numbers, his thoughts turned back to the huge fight he'd had with Carol that morning as he'd been about to walk out the door. Knowing he had a busy week planned, he'd told her not to count on him being home for dinner at all this week. She'd been furious, and a huge blow out had ensued. She believed that since he was now plant manager, he should be delegating more work to his employees so he could spend more time at home. She didn't want him "bucking the system" as she put it. She wanted him to cooperate more with management and "stop trying to change things that couldn't be changed". He fumed, thinking how she'd accused him of making more work for himself just for the sake of drama.

His jaw clenched as he thought back to the accident that had happened two months back. Now that was real drama. A visual image of twenty, and then as many as thirty, guys on the floor covered in blood flashed through his mind, and he realized what could have happened that day. If the compressor had come apart five or ten minutes earlier, before the bulk of the crew had gone on break, it could have been catastrophic. He shuddered at the mental images. The long line of ambulances lined up outside the gates, and news crews demanding answers and flashing pictures of the horrific scene on every television in Georgia. He shuddered at how much worse it easily could have been.

He still felt an overwhelming sense of guilt over the two men that were injured, and no one seemed to understand his feelings. He wasn't sure he could handle the guilt of more men being injured. He purposely shook his head, clearing the horrible images from his mind. He vowed to stay the course of making a change at Modern Products Manufacturing. Carol, management, and everybody else, would simply have to deal with it.

James purposely turned his attention back to his reports and, after a few moments of going over the numbers, was pleased to see the progress that had been made. The plan for transforming the plant was in full swing. The PM plan had been completed with over eight thousand components on a time-based refurbishment or replacement plan.

The Predictive (PdM) sub-team had also made progress. They had pulled three maintenance team members out of their jobs and had designated them "reliability specialists". They'd been trained on various inspection techniques and other technologies. Additionally, online monitoring had been set up on six critical pieces of equipment that the operators would watch continuously. The first five RCM teams would kick off next week, right on schedule.

James was also looking over the results of the plant assessment to date. As he expected, the Atlanta plant was rated poor on a number of measures. The results of the employee survey were particularly distressing. It was clear they were not getting the best out of their people. The answer to the final question was unnerving. Only 10% of the workforce answered positively to the question, "I actively look for ways to improve the plant." James ran his hand through his hair in frustration, knowing that it was virtually impossible to win a race when only 10% of the folks are doing the rowing.

To add insult to injury, this morning had felt like the "bad old days". James was pulled out of his HR reviews because of a failure on the number two line. The line was still down. He looked at his watch and realized that if it couldn't be brought back up within the next half hour, they would not be able to make their shipments that day. James hated having to make those kinds of calls to his customers.

He put the reports aside and decided he'd better go check out the progress personally. He walked out of his office and headed for the number two line. As he walked up to the line, he heard Vance cussing a blue streak. He stepped up behind him and stood there looking over his shoulder.

Vance, realizing James was there when he noticed people looking directly behind him with raised eyebrows, sheepishly looked up at James, knowing that he'd heard his tirade. James decided to ignore it. Vance, obviously frustrated, attempted to explain, "We've just ripped the line apart and found the culprit. The sling had been put in backwards. It was an easy mistake to make since neither the sling or the holder was well marked."

James nodded but kept quiet. He knew that what had Vance really ticked off was the fact that the sling had just been changed yesterday as part of the new PM plan. The phrase 'one step forward and two steps back' popped into James' head as he decided to hang around until the repair was completed, and the line brought back up. James glanced at his watch and was relieved that it looked like they were going to be able to make the production window after all.

Buzz, the operations manager, walked up and pulled James aside, finding a quiet spot a few yards away from the rest of the team.

"Thank God for Joe Miller and his maintenance team," Buzz stated. "I didn't think we had a prayer of getting this line up so fast. If you'd heard the god-awful noise it made right before it went down, you'd know what I mean. James, you need to do something big and showy for Joe. He really saved our bacon today. And it's not my place, but someone needs to sit down with that PM team and let them know they almost blew it for us today."

James crossed his arms, sighing out loud, as he leaned up against a corner of the wall. "Yeah, I guess you're right. I'll send a note to Joe and set him up for a cash award with HR." It was all James could muster as his thoughts centered on one comment Buzz had made that had him wondering.

"Let me ask you something though, Buzz. You said the line was making a noise before it went down?"

"Yeah, it started up right as the shift began," Buzz replied.

"Didn't you bring maintenance in?" James inquired, growing increasingly annoyed.

"Hell, no!" Buzz extorted. "We just brought the line down for them yesterday for their PM. We couldn't afford the down time. We thought we could make it to shift change."

James bit back his caustic retort, opting for diplomacy, but couldn't stop his head from shaking in frustration, or the sigh that escaped his lips. His formal communication system had failed again. At least twenty people had known there was a problem, and no one took action. How would they ever make any progress if this kind of crap continued?

Finally, at five pm, James sat down at his desk to review the plant score card. He had to admit it was hard to see any impact at this point, but it was still awfully early in the plan. He was not seeing the percent of planned work pick up at all.

Robert, from MRS, insisted that it soon would and when it did, it would be a good sign and an early predecessor to real financial results. He explained that the new planners had a lot of work to do in order to get the plans in the library created.

The other area of concern was cost. While raw materials cost was below the best in class, the labor cost was twice what it should be and so were the consumables, parts, and outside repairs. Overtime was also still up, which was a major problem when they were funding the MRS initiative. And, of course, the MRS bill was not small. All of the team-based work, extra inspections, planning, and scheduling work were driving a lot of hours. They were also using a lot more spare parts with the new PM regime. Although, not conducting PM's for a five year period turned out to be catastrophic in the case of the compressor that caused injury to his workers, it certainly had been cheaper.

Atlanta Scorecard 2 - December 3rd			
Key Performance Indicator	**Description**	**Atlanta Plant Current Year Forecast**	**Best in Class**
Maintenance as a % of Replacement Value	Maintenance cost, excluding capital compared to the estimated capital cost to replace the plant equipment	3.5%	2%
Overtime %	Percent of overtime for hourly workers	25%	<5%
Waste cost as a percent of raw materials cost	The cost of all scrap and defective output compared to total input	2.1%	0.2%
Raw material cost per ton of output	Applied only to plants making similar outputs	$18.73	$20
Labor cost per ton of output	Applied only to plants making similar outputs	$12.24	$7.30
Consumables, parts and outside repairs cost per ton		$5.41	$2.50
Energy costs per ton		$7.64	$7.25
% Planned Maintenance Work	% of work that is planned and scheduled at least 1 week in advance	0%	95%
Production % of Max	Maximum production the plant can operate at	81%	98%
Earnings	Last 12 months earnings in millions of dollars	$4.1 million (loss)	$40 million (profit)
Recordable injuries/ 200K man hours		2.55	<0.50

James had sent a copy of the plan, and the most recent results, to Chance and was eager to get his feedback. He had also received a pack of notes from him but had not had time yet to review them. He had hoped to talk to Chance earlier, but the hectic schedule with MRS had made it impossible. He picked up the phone and dialed Chance's number.

After the normal greetings, Chance didn't waste any time getting right to the heart of the matter. "Well, you guys sure have been busy down there in Atlanta," Chance chuckled.

"Yep," replied James proudly, "we're right on schedule with the implementation."

"I'm looking at the reports and it looks like you have a lot of PM's in place now."

"We sure do," James replied. "Preventive maintenance was the main focus of one of our teams."

"Have you ever stopped to think about why we do PMs?" Chance asked. "I mean the underlying assumptions that drive us to believe they are the right thing to do?"

James thought carefully, realizing that the question was fundamental, but he wasn't sure he knew the answer. He had spent the last eight weeks breaking his neck to put in the PM program and he couldn't answer such a basic question? No way was he going to admit that, he thought, as the silence became awkward.

"Well, Chance...," James answered cautiously, "PMs replace worn out parts before they cause a problem."

"That's my point. How do you know how frequently to replace them?" Chance asked.

It was clear Chance was trying to make a point, James thought, but he was at a loss as to what exactly that point was.

"Well, we generally rely on the manufacturer's recommendations, or when we have good data on the failure rate, we use our own data to set the time or cycles for the part," James replied.

"Exactly! So the replacement is done based on assumptions about time to failure, either based on actual data from the plant, or manufacturer's data. Either way, the implicit assumption is that defects come into the system primarily based on wear or time. Have you really explored that assumption?" Chance asked, without waiting for an answer. "I can tell you that in St. Louis, I had rotating equipment that ran for several years straight with only changes to lubrication. Let me ask a different question. If doing some PMs is good, wouldn't doing more PMs be better?"

This felt like a set-up to James but he wasn't sure how to answer. "Yeah, I guess so," he said hesitantly.

"Okay, so take me through the steps of doing a PM job," Chance replied.

James started, "Well, the job pops up on the schedule. We verify the plan for it and make sure the parts are in. Then we schedule the maintenance trades required and send them out with the work order. They take the equipment down..."

"It seems like your definition of a PM is to replace or repair worn parts," Chance interrupted. "I want to come back to that assumption in a second, but first, let me understand the current program. Your equipment can't be producing during a PM?"

"True, in most cases," James replied. "We can do basic inspections for wear, and there are some replacements that can be done in line or with spares, but most require shut downs." James was starting to see where this was headed.

"Well, what are your goals, James?" Chance asked bluntly.

"To get the plan implemented," James said, letting a little of his frustration show. This is not the conversation he'd expected to have.

"Really?" replied Chance. "I think you have your goals confused with your means."

"Huh?" was the only response James could muster.

"I guess you haven't read the material that I sent you, yet," said Chance.

James, feeling a little trapped, replied, "Well, as you know, things have been pretty hectic around here and..."

"Just do me a favor and pull out the top page," Chance interrupted. "This is how I thought about my priorities when I was in your shoes. It always helped to keep me from getting confused about what I was doing and why."

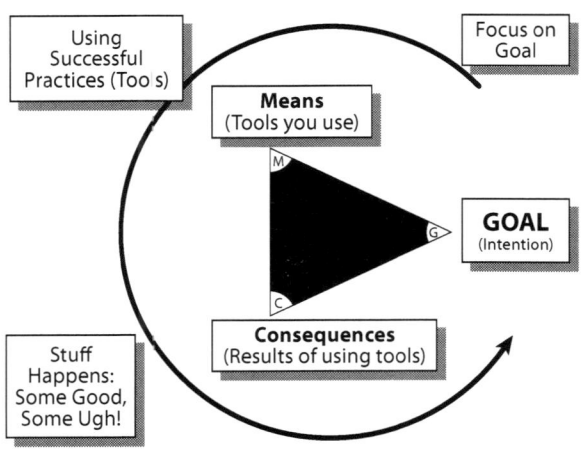

"You see," Chance continued, "I always thought the goal of my plant was to maximize production, meet my customers' needs, maintain my license to operate in the community and deliver value to the company. Now, there are all manner of tools to achieve those things, those are the means. Then, there are the things that fall out of chasing those goals and using those means, those are the consequences."

Chance went on to elaborate, "So, if the goal is to increase both throughput and added value, are PMs a helpful means or not? You're taking the equipment down when it could be running, reducing production, and swapping out parts that may or may not be bad, to accomplish a lower failure rate." Chance paused when James asked for a moment to take notes.

He continued, "To achieve your goals, it would seem to me that you want only the PMs that have a decent shot of eliminating a defect. PMs that don't eliminate a defect are simply wasting production and costing time and money. There is also a darker side. I have the first cut of the System Dynamics model back from the MIT folks, and there are two types of defects that could come in with any PM which create a potentially vicious feedback loop.

"First, there are defects that we'll call workmanship defects. These are imperfections that are introduced by the maintenance folks when they do a repair. When they do a job poorly, or don't have the right skills to do the job, they can introduce new defects. The second source of defects is from the parts we use. When parts are substandard, or simply wrong, they can also introduce defects. The MIT team has researched this, and the probability of adding those defects in any given job is over 15%, so your probability of taking a defect out better be higher than that or you're just going backwards."

James was processing all of this information as his thoughts turned to the situation with the oil sling on line two that morning. He wondered if the sling that had come out had had any defects in it.

"I see your point," James replied. "We shouldn't be adding PMs indiscriminately without really making sure that each one is effectively eliminating a defect. It all sounds great, but how exactly do we go about it?"

"What I used to do was have my maintenance team keep a log of defects found in replaced parts. If the find rate was low, we upped the time between PMs. From a Systems standpoint, the MIT team thinks of this as adding a balancing loop, where the goal is to minimize the total defects by adjusting the time between PMs. It takes a little longer for each job when you're checking the removed parts for defects, but it helped us lengthen the time between PMs, dramatically in some cases, and helped drive both real defect removal and production."

"Great point!" James replied, as the wheels started turning in his mind and all the possibilities sank in. James, suddenly energized, added, "I'll get my guys on this immediately."

"Now, let me challenge your definition of a PM. The purpose of a PM, in my mind, is to find and eliminate defects early on, before they become a problem. The third source of defects that I've been thinking about is what we called in St. Louis, aging. Unlike wine, defects don't get better with time. They get worse. You know the old saw by Benjamin Franklin that 'a stitch in time saves nine.' Today's little vibration is tomorrow's wobble and next week's catastrophic failure. Who does the PMs at your plant?" Chance asked.

"Well, that's maintenance's job. They're the only ones qualified to do the repairs," James added.

"Right, but they are not the most qualified to find defects. Your operators should be much better at that. After all, they operate the equipment. They know the ins and outs of how it runs and when something is a bit off. Maybe, if you rethink your PM program a bit, and allow operators to look for and eliminate small defects, you would see more results," Chance concluded.

"Uhm…,"James thought out loud, "that's a big change to a program we just got launched. Let me run it by the guys," James replied hesitantly.

"Can I ask you another question that's been bothering me?" James asked. "I can't seem to get the organization to communicate effectively. Everything reaches the front line very differently than the way I intend it. It's like one of those telephone games that kids play, where the final message bears only a passing resemblance to what you actually started with. I don't see how we're going to be effective with such poor communication. I'm not sure if I need to make personnel changes or what."

"I think I can help with that," Chance replied. "Instead of a long-winded answer now, let me write down some thoughts, send them to you, and we can discuss it later. I'd also like to find some time to walk you through the model and get your feedback. I'm hopeful that I can use it at other plants to explain the transition that you are going through in Atlanta. I think it will be ready to show in a month or so."

James was reluctant. He wanted to help Chance, but he had a lot of balls in the air right now. "Let me get back to you, Chance, but it would sure help if you could come down here in a couple of months. That would give us time to get our plan well under way."

As they were saying their good-byes, Chance added one last thing, "Make sure and talk to your front line supervisors in operations and maintenance regarding all of this planned work. They can give you the real story about how it is working. Don't count on that information percolating up. People are too invested in its success to give you the real feedback."

"I'll do that. Thanks again and I'll talk to you soon," replied James. He placed the phone in the receiver and sat for a long time, mulling over all the information Chance had provided.

By the time James finally left the office that evening, it was seven o'clock. He'd be home by seven-thirty, but the way he'd argued with Carol that morning, he sure didn't expect a plate of dinner left warming for him on the stove. He sighed as he got in the car and headed to the closest fast food drive-through on his way home.

Monday morning, James pulled his maintenance and operations managers, along with Robert, the lead MRS consultant, into an impromptu meeting. They joined him in the conference room, not knowing what to make of this meeting. It was clear that there was tension between Vance and Buzz, and that Robert was much more comfortable with Vance. James took a deep breath and began the meeting.

"Guys, I've been thinking about the PM program, and while I'm pleased with the program overall, I think we're ready for some tweaks. I'm concerned that the more PMs we do, the more likely we are to add new problems, like the oil sling last week. It's worth the risk if we're eliminating problems, but I'm not convinced that our replacement cycles are precise enough to know for sure. I'd like each crew doing a PM to also do an evaluation each time they complete a task to evaluate whether the PM eliminated a problem or not. I want both the area operations and maintenance supervisors to meet once a week to discuss whether we should lengthen the PM interval based on the results. I also want a weekly report on the PMs that changed so we can keep track of the results."

Buzz nodded in agreement, but Vance and Robert were looking at each other with puzzled expressions.

"Why do you want to lengthen the PM cycles?" Vance asked. "We just spent the last month getting them in place. If anything, we should be trying to get the number of PMs raised."

"If you lengthen the intervals, then we'll just go back to having failures," Robert added.

"I thought the same thing as late as yesterday, but the more I thought about it, the more I realized that conducting more PMs is not the goal, it's just a means to get more reliability and production. We want more effective PMs, not just more. Can you make my suggestions work?"

"Mmm....sure, I think so," answered Robert. "It's just a bit unorthodox is all. We'll have to spend more time per job, and our goal was to cut the maintenance time and cost."

"No," corrected James, "our goal is to make production, stay safe, and deliver value. Lower maintenance cost will be a consequence of doing that in the right way."

Robert shrugged and then nodded in agreement. They all started shuffling their papers and got up to leave the meeting. James was saving the operator PM concept for later. One battle at a time, he thought to himself, as he gathered up his own things and left the room.

That afternoon, an e-mail came in from Chance. In it, Chance had outlined his thoughts on effective communications. The gist of it was that formal communication networks (i.e., chain of command) were best for communications that help maintain order and the status quo. They were often very ineffective, even counterproductive, at communicating change. He cited several reasons from personal experience. First, many managers in the chain of command were vested in the status quo. They helped create it and were dependent on it for their careers. These managers tended to be poor communicators of change. Second, formal networks are slow and inaccurate in communicating cross-functionally. Typically, a message had to go up and then back down to get from one function to another. This hurt the speed of communications and allowed a lot of people to change or spin the message.

Chance recommended setting up a "shadow network" to focus on change. The shadow network would be made up of leaders who were inclined to pursue the goals and means that James and Chance had been talking about. Chance really emphasized the point that James needed to recruit the real leaders, and not just the managers who had the right titles. Intrigued, James picked up the phone to call Chance to discuss the shadow network idea in more detail. But Chance really threw James for a loop when he told him to go home and watch *The Wizard of Oz*.

"Yeah, right!" James replied, laughing out loud. "And then I'll watch *Mary Poppins* after that."

"No, I'm serious," Chance replied. "*The Wizard of Oz* is the classic Hero's Journey and I'm thinking you need a Hero's Journey right about now."

"What in the world are you talking about, Chance?"

"In Joseph Campbell's book, *The Hero with a Thousand Faces*, he states that the Hero's Journey represents the human experience of participating in an evolution to a higher state. It's also described as the process of achieving a higher level of being, and even though it's called the Hero's Journey, it's often done in groups, so it's frequently applied to the real world of organizational change. A number of people must commit to the journey and work together to advance the company to a higher operational level.

In order to successfully complete the journey, the heroes must travel an obstacle-filled path in their attempt to achieve a higher level. The journey takes time and commitment, and the heroes will face many trials, while many opportunities to abandon the call to change will arise. It's helpful to understand what will be faced before the journey begins so that these challenges can easily be overcome on the journey to a higher level of operation."

"Hmm, that's interesting. I've never even heard of the Hero's Journey."

"Well, the Hero's Journey is demonstrated in a number of literary works throughout the ages like *Jason and the Argonauts*, *King Arthur*, *The Wizard of Oz* and *Star Wars*. I spoke of gathering a group of people for your shadow network and that's just like Dorothy gathering her friends to travel with her down the yellow brick road in search of the Wizard of Oz."

"Okay....," James drew out skeptically.

"Listen, James. Here's something else to think about, ever hear of a chambered nautilus?"

"Yeah, sure, the shell, right?"

"Exactly, look up *The Chambered Nautilus* by Oliver Wendell Holmes. It really describes the journey you need to be on right now. You and your plant need to shed the old ways and create a new home with a new way of doing things, just like the nautilus. And in order to do that, you're going to have to fight a battle along the way. It's hard to get everyone on board and going down the same path you're traveling. You're always going to have the nay-sayers and the down right saboteurs getting in the way. So toughen up and get out your shield."

James laughed out loud, "My shield? As in my battle shield? Like in that movie, *300*?"

"That's a great example!" Chance exclaimed excitedly. "The soldiers were stronger when they united and locked their shields together."

James burst out laughing, "I just pictured Dorothy, the Tin Man, the Cowardly Lion, and Toto locking their shields together as they travel down the yellow brick road."

Chance barked out a laugh of his own, "Hey, whatever visualization works for you, James!"

James and Chance said their goodbyes. James hung up the phone with a great deal to contemplate. He wanted to check out that poem about the chambered nautilus, and he also planned to study up on the Hero's Journey, because he definitely needed to gather some allies. The shadow network was a great place to start, and it seemed like a great idea for the operator PM concept.

James knew just where to start - Reese Barnaby, the Extrusion line supervisor. Reese was short and round with a big Fu-man-chu mustache that was now almost completely gray. He was a no-nonsense guy who spoke his mind in a heavily drawled Southern accent. James always got a kick out of the phrases that Reese would use. He was a great leader, well respected and always open to improvement and new ideas.

He would need someone from maintenance as well. He immediately thought of Steve Sarkey, one of his best maintenance supervisors and a real go-getter. Steve was the exact opposite of Reese. He was skinny and bookish-looking with a long thin nose and narrow eyes. But, like Reese, he knew his stuff and was respected across the plant for his technical skill.

They would be the start of his shadow network. He set up a meeting for the next morning and asked them both to attend.

Over the last weeks of the year, and into the early months of the new year, James frequently met with Reese and Steve. He shared with them the ideas that were coming out of the sessions with Chance. They soaked it all up, and added their own thoughts here and there. Between the three of them, they put together a pilot operator PM and inspection program that Reese agreed to implement on the Extrusion line that he ran.

James was very pleased with how things were running and with how well his shadow network was working together. He'd read Joseph Campbell's book and watched the *Wizard of Oz* and *Star Wars* movies, seeing them in a whole new light. James had also developed an inspirational logo of sorts that he had his daughter, the computer wizard, as he affectionately called her, work up for him. It was a battle shield with a picture of a chambered nautilus on it. He had it posted on his bulletin board in his office. Whenever he doubted himself, or needed inspiration, he pictured that shield.

His own Hero's Journey had begun, and he was excited to see how it would all play out.

A Dismal Success

Seven months after the accident, on his way to work early one beautiful May morning, James reviewed his schedule while stopped at a traffic light. He was pleased to see that although he was very busy, and had a meeting scheduled with his management team that day, he still had plenty of open spaces throughout the day to tend to any unforeseen problems that might arise.

He moved forward in traffic with a smile on his face, pleased at the thought that his day would be one of those smooth-running days he had been enjoying more and more frequently. He was pleased at how well things had been running lately. They had even found the energy to start the implementation of the new CMMS system. They were on an upward swing, and James felt confident that there were no more accidents in their future.

James then thought of Carol. It had been a tough few months for his family. His wife had complained that she felt like a single parent. However, when he explained his overwhelming sense of responsibility for the accident, her anger had deflated and turned to compassion as she patted his shoulder. He knew he was very lucky to have such an understanding wife. After that conversation, she had stoically taken care of the house and the family with no complaints. If there were problems, he never heard about them, and he really appreciated that. Things were getting better now, and he had been making a conscious effort to spend more time with the family.

As he entered the plant, he greeted his employees in the break room, anticipating having the time to sit down and drink a cup of coffee before starting his day. Unfortunately, one of his leaders stopped by to ask him for a quick meeting about a piece of equipment that had broken down overnight. He sighed as he left his mug by the sink and made his way to the supervisor's office.

Once James finally made it into his office, he plopped down into the chair at his desk. The change effort had been in progress for six months now. He couldn't believe he was in his office at six o'clock in the morning, but he needed to go over some reports before his meeting. The reports indicated that the results from the planned maintenance efforts were still mixed. Robert, the consultant from MRS, had been crowing about how they had nailed each of the milestones and the plan was perfectly on schedule. James had to admit that they had executed the plan like clockwork. However, the results were still lagging. Costs were totally out of control, and he wouldn't be able to hide that for long. The initial jump that he had seen in the percent of planned work, production, and the serenity of less reactive work, had been steadily slipping over the last few weeks.

After sifting through the many e-mail messages in his inbox, he saw that meetings filled most of the empty slots in his schedule. Well, at least he would still make it home in time to catch his son's baseball game.

He reflected back to that dreadful day, nearly seven months ago, and realized how blessed he was to have such a good group of people working for him who were now more confident and thorough. He liked how they were bringing solutions to the table, rather than problems.

It all had to do with the implementation of the new planned maintenance strategy he had finally shared with everyone. They had had the plan in action for a while now, but he was beginning to sense that there were some underlying problems he wasn't hearing about. He couldn't quite put his finger on exactly what it was, but something was off kilter and he couldn't figure it out. It was almost as if Vance was taking advantage of his power by not letting others make decisions and keeping things close to the vest.

Then there was the Computerized Maintenance Management System (CMMS) or the 'Consultant Money Making System' as the plant employees called it when they thought he couldn't hear. It had been nothing short of a disaster.

The old system could not handle all of the new types of work: planning, scheduling, PMs, inspections, and RCMs. More than ever, James saw the need for the system, but that was not the issue. The process of putting it in, gathering the data, and redefining their equipment hierarchy was overwhelming. More and more time was being sucked away from the operations, maintenance, and engineering teams to feed the new system the data it required. To cut the time and cost, they were now seriously considering not loading any historical data. This seemed crazy to James. If they didn't load their historical data, it would take another two to three years before they would have adequate data in the system.

Of course, all of the time committed so far did not include the upcoming training on the new system for everyone at the plant. What a catch twenty-two, James thought. He knew they needed to have a system to put in planned maintenance, but getting the system installed was taking so much time from the resources required to do planned maintenance that it was jeopardizing the program.

Robert and the formal network were blaming each other for the problems, and each person assured James that they had done their part according to the plan.

Not that it was all bad news. The operator PM program that Chance had recommended was working brilliantly. Steve and Reese had worked with the team and come up with a checklist that each shift used to inspect for defects and make minor adjustments. Steve had a 'quick response' resource designated on his maintenance team who would come and fix any defects that the operators could not tackle themselves.

The Extrusion line had never looked or operated better. The operators and mechanics had thoroughly cleaned in and around the equipment after Reese had reminded them, "You can't kill a defect you can't see." James especially liked the concept of killing defects. After all, that's what those pesky things were trying to do to his plant.

The team had also set up a number of simple but ingenious devices to be able to spot defects quickly. All of the dials on the gauges had been rotated so that straight up and down meant normal operations. Even James, who was by no means an expert on the Extrusion line, could walk through and quickly tell how things were running in one glance. All of the nuts on the rotating equipment had match marks to the base plate that clearly showed when they were properly torqued, and all of the grease fittings were color coded to ensure that the right grease was used in each application. The cooperation and the ingenuity were all very exciting, but the results were what grabbed James' attention.

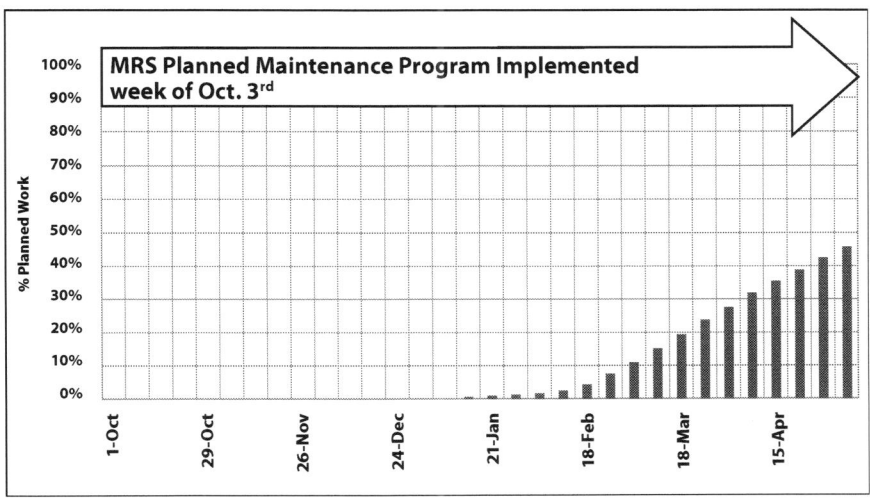

Reactive call outs in the area were down 30% in the past month as were related costs. Planned maintenance was climbing every week and was the highest for any area in the Atlanta plant. It was now up to 46% and increasing about 10% each month. Production availability for the Extrusion line was up from the low 80% range to over 90%.

However, this last improvement was a bit of a frustration for James. After all, the Extrusion line was not the plant's bottleneck. More production in that area was not providing him more overall volume or sales. The overall plant production was still stuck at 81% capacity, and he was kicking himself for not starting in the bottleneck areas. Although, he reminded himself, in those areas of the plant he did not have someone like Reese.

Atlanta Scorecard 3: May 6th			
Key Performance Indicator	Description	Atlanta Plant Current Year Forecast	Best in Class
Maintenance as a % of Replacement Value	Maintenance cost, excluding capital compared to the estimated capital cost to replace the plant equipment	4.0%	2%
Overtime %	Percent of overtime for hourly workers	31%	<5%
Waste cost as a percent of raw materials cost	The cost of all scrap and defective output compared to total input	2.2%	0.2%
Raw material cost per ton of output	Applied to only plants making similar outputs	$18.71	$20
Labor cost per ton of output	Applied to only plants making similar outputs	$13.13	$7.30
Consumables, parts and outside repairs cost per ton		$6.08	$2.50
Energy costs per ton		$7.65	$7.25
% Planned Maintenance Work	% of work that is planned and scheduled at least 1 week in advance	46%	95%
Production % of Max	Maximum production the plant can operate at	81%	98%
Earnings	Last 12 months earnings in millions of dollars	$4.2 million (loss)	$40 million (profit)
Recordable injuries/ 200K man hours		2.77	<0.50

He wondered which was more important to get started, the biggest production opportunity or the most fertile ground for change. The engineer in him told him to focus on the bottleneck, but that same voice in his head had told him that the planned maintenance plan would work flawlessly. While the losses were the same today as when the MRS program first started six months ago, the losses topped four million dollars per year.

The production that week had dropped to 76% of capacity because of all the extra downtime spent conducting the planned maintenance. It was no wonder Buzz wasn't willing to cooperate in taking the equipment down. They were making a nice comeback, but he wasn't sure if the improvements would continue. If the plant didn't become profitable soon, he just might be out of a job. He made a note to bring it up with Chance in their next private conversation.

Fortunately, James had his shadow network which had now grown to ten people, mostly first line supervisors, a couple of operators from the Extrusion line, and a couple of enthusiastic engineers. From the information gathered through his shadow network, James was getting a clearer picture of what was going wrong. Everything else had been going well, specifically in the area of communication, so he shrugged off his concerns and went back to his e-mails.

At seven o'clock, James glanced at his watch, hurriedly gathered up his files, and headed for the conference room. He had scheduled an early morning meeting so it would not disrupt too much of their daily work. Chance had come for the meeting and had brought Mark Sterman, the professor from MIT, and his research assistant. They were going to show the team the results of the modeling in hopes that it would help drive any changes to the plan. Together, they were going to come to some conclusions on what was going wrong and how to fix it.

Yesterday, James had sent out an e-mail listing the agenda for this morning's meeting:

1. Recap of the planned maintenance efforts - what is working, what is not, and why
2. Recap of operator PM program and next steps
3. System Dynamics introduction
4. Review the System Dynamics model

James walked into the conference room, greeted everyone, and sat down. When everyone was seated, he started off the meeting, "As you all know, this is an informal group, and everyone is encouraged to participate. However, we are not here to decide official policy. We're hoping to better understand what is working and what isn't." With that, he turned to Steve, the bookish maintenance supervisor that he had recruited to be in the shadow network, and asked for a recap of the PM and PdM programs.

Steve looked at his notes, then began, "Well, it seems that the number of preventive and predictive planned jobs has slipped a good bit from last month. In some ways, that's good. A full 5% have gone away because we lengthened the intervals on some PMs when we discovered that no defects were being found. However, I'm hearing more and more often from mechanics that they are not being given the equipment by the operations team. Reese, do you have any insight into that?"

Reese sat up and glanced around with obvious trepidation, "We can still say anything in this session, right?" When James nodded, Reese continued, "Well, what Steve said is true. There have been a number of jobs that my peers and I have refused to schedule. We have been under so much pressure to make production from James and Buzz that we simply couldn't afford the downtime."

James felt his defenses rising. It was true enough that he was pressing Buzz and the operations team hard, but with good reason. The sales group had just landed a new customer, and the extra volume would do wonders for the plant's profitability, however, it would be a stretch to hit the new weekly production numbers.

"It's true, I have put pressure on production, but I certainly never meant to short change our planned program. If you recall, when we started this program, this was not supposed to be a trade-off. The planned maintenance was supposed to increase our capacity."

"Exactly," added Steve. "We can't expect this program to work if we're not willing to take the risk to actually do it. And frankly, the maintenance team is getting pretty frustrated. So much work has gone into creating the PMs, training on inspections, not to mention all of the planning that goes into each job, that when the operators refuse to give us the equipment, it just feels like a gigantic waste of time. I'll be honest. There are a number of folks in maintenance who just want to go back to fire fighting. They're busting their butts in this new program only to find that we're still running things to failure like before. It was a lot less work to just fix it when it broke."

James sputtered and started to reply, but before James could get anything out, Steve interrupted, "Let me give just one example, if I could. Two weeks ago, the vibration specialist picked up an abnormal vibration in one of the Extrusion line's main drive motors. We planned the job, went to operations to schedule it, and they deferred it. We tracked the vibration, which got increasingly worse, and sure enough it failed this last Sunday. I had to call in guys on their day off, and they worked well into the night. To top it off, when the motor seized, it bent the drive shaft. So, the fix that would originally have taken two hours and about twenty-five dollars in parts, took almost eight hours and cost over two hundred dollars. Now, how does that make any sense on something we knew had a defect?"

Reese asked, "James, you tell me, because I'll do it whichever way you say, boss. If I'm faced with a trade-off of making the week's production numbers, or sticking with the planned maintenance schedule, what is the right decision? Everything that Steve is saying is true, but I couldn't afford the two hours that week."

James pondered the question. It was a fair question. Which of the two was the higher priority? He hated to send mixed messages, but finally he answered, "You have to make the production number."

Chance interrupted, "If I can make an observation. This is a classic problem, and I am afraid there is no easy answer. I'm sure all of you feel that the planned maintenance program is more important for the long term success of the plant but making this week's shipments will always be more urgent. In the end, urgent almost always beats important. For every inspection that shows a defect, sometimes it will fail, just like you predict, but many times it will make it one more shift, or day, or week. And so, we roll the dice and take our chances. But collectively, these decisions pull us out of the planned maintenance mode and right back to reacting. The only way to win is to create some buffer for yourself so that you don't have to trade-off the 'important' for the 'urgent'. Are there any ways to do that in this situation?"

They discussed it for a few minutes and came up with a couple of solutions that could help in the short term. They decided that they would run a couple of weekend shifts to get ahead of demand and accumulate some finished product. They would also tap into a sister plant with capacity across the country. Both would add some small costs temporarily but would break the cycle of the "urgent" versus the "important" dilemma.

With a look of frustration, Vance, the maintenance manager, challenged the group, "Look, I'm confused. Doesn't this violate everything that we learned over the last year about lean manufacturing? I mean we all went to those workshops. Wasn't the goal to eliminate buffers and reduce inventory?"

"No, no, no," Chance replied. "That is not the goal. Reduced inventory is the consequence of reduced variability. Sure, you want to reduce inventory somewhat to expose the problems. I would say that right now your variability issues are well exposed."

When Vance had been somewhat appeased, James turned the meeting over to Cindy, one of the engineers in the network, and asked her to give an update on the RCM program.

Cindy started with a sigh, "Do you want the good news or the bad news first?" Everyone chuckled nervously as Cindy continued, "We completed fifteen comprehensive RCMs on equipment that was either critical to production or expensive to repair. We had cross functional teams on each, with at least one engineer and an experienced facilitator from MRS. We cataloged over 1500 failure modes, assessed the risk, and then created an appropriate plan for each. That's the good news. The bad news is that the binders for these fifteen studies are now primarily wall decorations in my boss' office. We've made almost no progress on actually implementing the suggested actions."

"Well, that's really news to me. I had no idea that so many were complete," Steve replied.

"I don't know why you say that, Steve. People from your maintenance team were on several of the RCM teams," Cindy shot back.

"Yeah, I know, but I asked them about the progress and they told me that the meetings had stopped."

"Well, the engineers and facilitators were finishing up the recommended actions, and we didn't want to waste the front line's time with those details," Cindy replied.

"For the Extrusion line, if we implemented all of the recommendations, how many new work orders a week are we talking about?" inquired Reese.

Cindy took a minute to consult her notes and answered, "It looks like about one hundred."

"One hundred!?" shouted Reese. "Are you serious? There is no way we can handle that. Weren't you listening to the last half hour's discussion? We're going to have to start over and rethink that list."

Cindy and James groaned at the same time. They had already invested a great deal of engineering and consulting time in the analysis, only to hear now that they needed more analysis.

"Thanks, Cindy. Let's table that discussion, and I'll follow up with Robert after the meeting," James said, wanting to wrap up that topic before it sucked all of the positive energy from the network.

They spent the next fifteen minutes with Reese, the Extrusion line supervisor, going over the progress and results of the operator PM program. The energy in the room was coming up again. James ended the topic by stating that they would take the program to another area in the plant starting next week and would need the network's help to get it done.

James took the floor next to give an update on the progress of the CMMS implementation. He detailed the issues with collecting and validating data on equipment, the efforts to come up with an equipment and component hierarchy, and the debate about whether to carry historical data or not. When he finished no one knew quite what to say. There seemed to be no good answers on how to fix the issues.

Finally, Chance chimed in, "I don't have an answer, but your whole description reminds me of an old Peter Drucker quote, 'Nothing is less productive than to make more efficient what should not be done at all.'

"Can I tell you guys a story that one of my mentors shared with me when I was struggling with a particularly tough patch in my career?" Chance asked. He continued without waiting for an answer, "It seems there was this fellow who lived in a valley, and he had trading to do with a village in a nearby valley. However, between the two villages there was quite a large mountain. The man sized up the situation and saw clearly that the most direct route to the other village was right over that mountain. So for some time, he loaded up his pack and hiked over that rugged mountain pass to do his trading. Now, it happened that there was also a lady in the village where this man lived who also wanted to trade with the village on the other side of the mountain. However, when she sized up the situation, she saw that the easiest way to the village was around the mountain. Oh sure, it was longer, but it was flat and the road was smooth and reliable. One day, the two met and began discussing their trading, and their approaches to get to the other village. The man ridiculed the woman for taking such an indirect route, but she convinced him to give it a try on his next trip. The man was astonished. He arrived at the same village, in less time and with less effort, by taking what seemed to be a longer route."

James stared at Chance with a bemused expression. He glanced around the table and noticed similar looks on the faces of the others. What was the purpose of the story? What was it supposed to mean, and what was Chance implying? He wondered if Chance thought they should just scrap the CMMS system, or scrap the whole planned maintenance effort. Sure, easy for him to say when it's not his neck on the line for performance. He hasn't lived through the last seven months of pain getting it to where it is now. With his annoyance growing, James decided to avoid the topic all together and shifted gears to the next item on the agenda.

He turned the meeting over to Mark Sterman, the professor from MIT, by giving a quick recap of Mark's background and the scope and purpose of the study. After brief introductions, Mark said, "Instead of a dry academic version of what System Dynamics is about, I thought we could play a game that will clearly illustrate the principles. It's called the Beer Distribution Game[1], but I can assure you that there is no actual beer drinking involved, especially not at this hour in the day. I am going to break you into two teams, and you are going to compete as two distinct beer distribution systems."

For the next hour and a half, the group had a lot of fun. They were running a beer supply chain where a consumer's demand for beer

[1] An on line version of The beer distribution simulator can be viewed at web.mit.edu/jsterman/www/SDG/MFS/simple-beer.html

was revealed weekly to the retailer. The retailer then ordered from the wholesaler and received product. The wholesaler then ordered from a distributor, who in turn ordered from a manufacturer. Each time the beer order passed through a supplier, there was a delay. There was a penalty for holding too much inventory and a bigger one for running out of the beer swilling customer's favorite beverage. The whole distribution system was represented on a paper game board that was five feet long and had boxes and lines representing the flows of product and information. The cases of beer were represented with pennies.

It seemed that beer demand was highly cyclical in this game. The final customer was swinging from beer-guzzling couch potato to tea-totaling goody-goody almost week to week. James was not sure what lesson they were learning, but it was great to see the team having some fun after the last seven months. When they were finished with the simulation and had shown their see-saw graphs of demand, their customer disappointing stock-outs, and their warehouse packed with an oversupply of inventory, Mark Sterman asked everyone to describe what happened. Everyone blamed the unreliable consumer, and the inherent cyclicality built into demand. If only demand had been more stable, they certainly would have performed better.

Mark had cautioned the retailers to conceal consumer demand. He now asked them to reveal actual consumer demand. The consumers had made one change in demand the entire simulation with a single spike that had remained level for the rest of the game.

James was dumbfounded. If the consumer was not to blame for all of the gyrations in the system, who was? Mark went on to explain that their results were very typical. All of the cycles of booms and busts in the simulation were caused by the decisions of the participants and the structure of the system itself. The feedback loops, like the reorder cycle, the inherent time delays, and managers' perceptions and misperceptions about those dynamics caused the behavior.

Mark, the professor, was getting more and more excited as he tied these simulated results to the real world. He pointed out the decision rules and blind spots of participants. He moved from the virtual supply chain laid out on the table, to the tracking charts on the wall, to the overhead projector, where he had actual data from industry that looked eerily like the graphs they had just produced in the game.

The conclusion, he explained, was "structure creates behavior." He waited a minute for effect and then repeated, "Structure creates behavior! Many of the events that seem to be random or out of our control are, in fact, from a systems perspective, a direct result of the decisions we make and the structure of the system we are in. The only way to change the result is to understand the structure and make different decisions, or change the structure."

It was the perfect introduction to the modeling work, James thought, as he looked around the room and saw that everyone was engaged. They all wanted to understand the structure of the Atlanta Plant system and how it was creating the behavior they were all so desperately trying to change.

Mark continued, "We believe that the engine that really drives this system's behavior is the introduction and elimination of defects from the system. Chance has kept us in the loop with his ongoing conversation about the sources of defects, and we have incorporated that into the model. As you know, there are seven sources of defects, and five are primary drivers."

With that final note, Mark projected a slide onto the screen in the conference room and proceeded to walk them through it. James was pleased to see that each team member was engaged and listening attentively. Mark then discussed each point to make sure it was clear to all of them.

He put up a slide titled, *"Workmanship"*, and explained. "These defects were introduced by the maintenance team when they didn't repair equipment properly. The backwards oil sling installation, from a couple of months back, is a classic example. The team has been debating whether these defects come from skill issues, not being given the proper time to do a job, or simply pride in one's work. In the end, the conclusion was that all of the above could be potential reasons."

Mark then put up a slide titled, *"Poor Operating Practices"*. He paused before continuing, giving everyone a chance to soak in the title. "It's clear that some defects come from the way the plant is operated."

James had just heard an example of this in the Extrusion line operating with a known vibration. The way operators ran their equipment made a huge difference on the defects introduced. It took a while for Reese to come around on this one. Other than normal wear and tear, he did not see how operators added additional defects. The clincher had been when Cindy, who was a neighbor of his, asked him how many clutches he had replaced in his teenage son's car. When Reese replied that it had been three in the last two years, Cindy folded her arms and raised her eyebrows.

Mark put up the next slide, which had the title, *"Bad Parts"*, and cleared his throat before continuing. "When the replacement parts used are poor or inappropriate for the job, defects are introduced. This occurs for a number of reasons. For instance, it's difficult to have exactly the correct part for an unplanned job, so maintenance often improvises. Prior cost cutting initiatives could lead to purchases of substandard parts, and sometimes defects can be introduced by improper storage or transportation."

There was a little murmuring in the back and a lot of nodding going on as the next slide titled, *"Normal Wear"*, was put up. "In almost all cases, the act of operating the equipment, and sometimes simple exposure to the elements, will wear equipment and result in defects."

Everyone bought into this concept immediately. It was clear to James that he and the team believed this to be the leading source of defects. After all, everyone could name specific examples of a belt wearing, a bearing wearing out, or a pipe corroding over time. Chance, in his usual counterintuitive way, acknowledged these defects but argued that wear was not the only factor. It was very clear that he did not believe it was the leading source of defects.

"Design", was the next slide title that appeared, as Mark took a quick drink of water before continuing. "Defects are also created when equipment is not designed properly for its function. If equipment is undersized, the wrong metallurgy, overpowered, or otherwise ill-designed, failures can result."

There were certainly plenty of design defects in new equipment. But the team had talked about the fact that often design defects crept in as the market and plant changed. Things that were designed perfectly on day one could suddenly have a design defect if the application changed.

"Cindy gave me a great example," Mark said. "The old Extrusion line was still in operation to handle orders that only the less automated process could handle. However, the volume had fallen to less than 10% of the designed capacity. Suddenly, the team was faced with a rash of failures. It turned out that the line was never designed to move that little volume, and several components were literally tearing themselves apart at the lower output. No amount of maintenance, or adherence to operating standards, would have fixed the problem. They had to fix the design defect to eliminate the failures."

When Mark saw that there were no further questions, he added, "The first three defects can create a reinforcing loop that may really help or hurt the system. More reactive work leads to more repairs and therefore more opportunities for workmanship and parts defects. At the same time, poor availability can lead to cutting corners or deferring repairs in operations that can, in turn, create more defects."

Mark then put up another slide. "There are two other sources of defects that are secondary effects. The first is *"Aging"*. As Chance described earlier, defects don't typically get better with time. They tend to get worse. Small defects left in the system get bigger, or spawn new defects, because they are left alone. That's the whole theory behind the pilot operator PM program. The success of that program shows how powerful it can be to eliminate this source of defects.

"Another source of defects is *"Failure"*. While defects cause failures when they get bad enough, failures can also create defects. Failures often result in vast amounts of energy being misdirected in machinery. That energy often causes new defects." As Mark continued to explain, he reminded them of Steve's earlier story about the motor that froze and bent the shaft, and how the failure of the motor caused a defect in the shaft.

Mark paused before adding one last thought, "These are clearly both self-reinforcing feedback loops."

The discussion continued for some time, and a fairly lively debate broke out, with the team arguing about which sources were the most important and therefore the ones that they should take action on. If the team was right, and Chance was wrong, about wear being the main culprit, then the best course of action would be some re-engineering of the equipment and some capital upgrades to make it wear slower. They debated how they could determine the sources.

Chance chimed in, "Why don't you just ask the equipment?" Everyone laughed, and Chance allowed the room to quiet down before continuing, "No, really, the equipment knows how it's been run, how it's been repaired, and how it has failed in the past. Your operating and work order system tracks most of those events. Why don't you do a forensic defect analysis and look at the last five hundred to one thousand work orders? You could also interview the people involved, if you need to, and determine the source of the defect. Even if it's not perfect, it will give you a ball park area to focus on."

Everyone, looking intrigued, discussed the possibilities, and it was decided this was an excellent way to figure out where to focus. They discussed and refined the concept of the audit.

Cindy, the engineer, suggested doing a simple root cause analysis on each failure to get at the source, and Steve volunteered to lead the effort. James was thrilled with the progress of the meeting and feeling quite smug as he leaned back in his chair.

Mark continued, "Well, now that we've settled that, let's go on. Most of the rest of the model is a set of balancing loops that have the dual, and often competing, goals of maximizing production through the elimination of defects and the minimization of costs. How the model performs depends largely on what policies are followed and how effectively defects are removed. It also depends on what policies are in place balancing cost and production and what the rate of defect introduction is."

They spent over an hour going through the rest of the model in detail as Mark explained the connections that the MIT folks had made based on the interviews. The team made a lot of suggestions with regard to where they thought the policies and data did not reflect reality. The model was set up so that Mark could plug a bunch of policies into the front-end, such as how many planners to have and what level of PMs to do, then run a scenario to gauge results. The team went back and forth between understanding the model and running scenarios to see the impact of different decisions. On one of the runs, James noticed that Mark had a saved scenario called "Halve the Defect Introduction Rate". James, puzzled, asked him about it.

"Oh, we were just having some fun back at the University. We noticed all of the self-reinforcing feedback loops in the defect generation area. We thought it would be interesting to see, if it was possible to wave a magic wand and cut the defect rates in half, how the system would perform. I can show you the results if you're interested."

James, intrigued, nodded his agreement, and Mark opened the scenario. It took James a minute to re-orient to the numbers. None of the policies that they had looked at all morning had more than a 10% variance in overall plant results, much to James' frustration. This scenario, however, was showing dramatic improvements to production, cost, and almost every other major metric.

James sat back and laughed out loud. "That sure would seem to be a very valuable magic wand."

Chance smiled and replied with a self satisfied smirk, "Indeed."

Finally, at ten-thirty, the meeting was winding down. James thanked everyone for participating, and as everyone was filing out, he and Chance agreed to reconnect the next morning.

James had planned a leisurely lunch at the local restaurant with his department heads. He was treating them to a nice lunch in order to thank them for all the hard work they had been putting in, but as he was preparing to head out the door, one of his leaders requested a quick meeting to discuss an operations scheduling problem due to a pump that had just gone out.

James sighed in frustration, wondering why it had been such a bad day for equipment failures. They had moved from reactive mode to more of a planned mode, but today was certainly a reactive day, and it was playing havoc with his schedule, not to mention his nerves. Equipment failures made him nervous. What if another accident happened?

He felt his heart rate increase as he picked up the phone to let everyone know he wouldn't be able to join them for lunch as he'd planned. He gave Vance his company credit card to pay for lunch and asked them to bring him back a burger from the restaurant. He had more important issues to deal with.

By the end of the day, he was definitely feeling frazzled. It was five o'clock, and he had a few other things to finish before he could leave. He sighed, resigning himself to the fact that he would be missing the first half of his son's game. Tommy would be disappointed, and Carol would guilt him with one of her looks. She was growing increasingly more impatient with the amount of time he was spending at work.

He thought about all the equipment failures that had caused problems for him today and realized that their defect elimination campaign was obviously just beginning. He felt torn between his family obligations and handling problems at the plant, but in the end, he knew there was really no decision to make at all. Safety had to come first. He just hoped he still had a family by the time he had the plant straightened out.

By the end of the week, more equipment had failed, and James felt like he had gone back in time to being a reactive leader. He decided to call Vance in for a meeting after he discovered that inspections had recently dropped off.

James asked his assistant, Lorraine, to find Vance and ask him to report immediately to his office. James sat back in his chair, awaiting Vance's arrival, going over in his head exactly what he wanted to say. James knew he would have to be careful since Vance tended to be pretty prickly these days. James sat up when Vance, looking harried, entered James' office without knocking.

"Lorraine said you needed me?"

"Yes, Vance, I'm very concerned about the inspection numbers," James stated, getting right down to business.

Vance snorted and shot back, "Well, James, inspections were only turning up with a problem about 3% of the time, and I felt that all those inspections were a waste of time."

James' mouth hung open in shock. This was exactly what Sterman had predicted with the use of his model. "So you just cut back on inspections?" James asked in frustration. James was so upset that he had to bite his tongue not to add a few choice words like "you stupid idiot" to the end of his question.

James thought back to Mark Sterman's warning when they were going over the computer model. In the model, in order to reach a high level of planned maintenance, they had to increase the inspections to the point where inspectors found defects only 3% of the time. Which was exactly the number Vance just threw out and precisely reinforced Sterman's theory. In fact, Sterman's theory was that the reason so many planned maintenance programs failed was because it was very difficult to keep people inspecting at that high rate.

Sterman had talked about how demoralizing it was for people to do work that only saw results 3% of the time. Everyone tended to want to quit doing inspections, but Sterman was adamant that it was vital to stay the course. He did point out, however, that only highly autocratic managers were able to enforce that high a level of inspections. James couldn't understand why Vance wasn't using his naturally autocratic nature to do more inspections rather than less.

Sterman had also pointed out that there was only one case in his studies, of a manager from Alumax, who was strong enough to persevere through that road block for a long period of time. James really didn't plan on going the Alumax route. He was much more interested in collaboration of workers rather than a top down control philosophy.

Before Vance could answer his question, James continued, "Well, Vance, I need you to know that I'm holding you personally responsible for all the equipment problems we've been having lately. So where do we go from here?"

Vance visibly bristled, gave some vague non-answers, looked at his watch, and stated, "I have an appointment, so I've got to run."

James didn't feel that anything had really been resolved, but he followed him out the door, letting the matter go for now. Vance stomped past Lorraine's desk so quickly, he left Lorraine sputtering with her mouth hanging open and her arm raised in an attempt to get his attention. Lorraine's prudish, "Well, I never...," had James attempting to hide his amused grin behind his hand as he leaned against the door jamb of his office door.

Lorraine turned around in her chair and skewered James with a scowl, "What was he all fired up about? Goodness, James, do you have to get everyone all riled up? I had a question for him about this report you asked me to do. I just don't know how I can possibly be expected to get anything done around here with everyone stomping around acting like children."

James smiled, shrugging his shoulders in mock confusion.

Lorraine rolled her eyes and stated, "You men, always running around, creating havoc, and making more work for everyone else."

James mentally cringed at her words, which sounded eerily similar to complaints he'd heard from his wife, but he laughed knowing Lorraine was all bark. "Now, Lorraine, you're starting to sound just like my wife."

Lorraine let out a loud "humph" and mumbled something under her breath he was sure he didn't want to hear anyway. He simply smiled as she purposely ignored him and started re-arranging her desk.

On Monday morning, James was greeted in his office by Vance. Over the last few months, he had found Vance increasingly more difficult to work with. Vance was a great maintenance manager and a nice person, but the planned maintenance program, and the resulting power it gave him, had obviously gone to his head. He was constantly challenging people and using the implicit threat of not complying with the corporate maintenance program to bully them into doing what he wanted.

Vance asked, "James, can I get a minute of your time."

From the look on Vance's face, and his tone, James could tell it was not going to be a pleasant conversation. "Sure, Vance, what's on your mind?"

"Well, I have been working on getting the inspections back up like you wanted, but we're having a lot of trouble getting operations to cooperate with the planned maintenance program. Buzz and his team keep prioritizing the production schedule over the program. Don't get me wrong, I understand we need to make production, but we're slipping backwards on this program. I know it's a huge priority with Jennings and the folks at Corporate, but I think we need to create a consolidated schedule that includes the maintenance program. You, Buzz, and I can decide weekly what the priorities will be. By the way, Robert, and the other folks at MRS, agree with me on this."

James felt a tic in his cheek as his jaw clenched. Not only was Vance being a pain in the butt, but the fact that he'd gone behind his back to get the others' supposed agreement really didn't sit well with him. He tempered the response he wanted to give and gave a more diplomatic one.

"I will take it under advisement, but realize that, even with a committee, it will be hard to make the decision any other way. Jennings wants this program done, but it will only take one call from an irate customer who doesn't get their shipment for him to adjust his priorities. I have some ideas on how we can get some buffer capacity over the next few weeks to handle both priorities. Steve and Reese are helping to pull those together this morning."

Vance shuffled a bit, staring down at his feet, before he looked back up at James. "That's the other thing that I wanted to talk with you about. I've noticed that Steve has been working on quite a few special projects for you lately, and I wasn't made aware of what he's working on. I was just hoping you would enlighten me."

James mentally groaned, knowing that Vance was not going to play nice when it came to their little network. He mentally grabbed for a plausible answer, "Well, I've given him a few projects to work on, but it's nothing that should get in the way of his normal duties. Let me know if it does."

James hoped his last remark was enough of a dismissal, without seeming rude, as he turned back to his computer. He really did not want to go into details with Vance.

"Well, actually, it is getting in the way", Vance persisted as he walked further into the office and sat in the chair in front of James' desk. "I understand that you have him putting in an alternative PM program, and he's been working on what he calls defect elimination. This morning, when I asked him to review this week's inspections, he told me he needed to work on a source of defects project for you. James, I can't run my team if you're re-assigning them and giving them other tasks. All of this defect work is getting in the way of getting the planned maintenance work done."

James sighed, pushing back in his chair. Obviously, Vance was not going to let it go. "Vance, you know as well as I do that the planned program is struggling. I'm trying to use Steve, and a few others, to really understand what is working, what is not working, and why, from a ground up perspective. Have you seen the results of the operator PM program? It's the best thing we have going." James hoped his answer would appease Vance.

"Yeah, I saw them and reviewed them with Robert. He's convinced the only difference in results comes from the fact that the operators are allowing these PMs to happen. We would have results like that if they would simply implement the program. If Steve were doing his job instead of all these projects, we might actually make some headway," Vance argued defiantly.

James felt the last sentence had been thrown out as a challenge and knew things were boiling to a head, but he felt powerless to stop it. James started to answer but was cut off.

"I just don't see where you are going with this defect stuff. We have a plan to turn the plant around based on solid benchmark data, an experienced consultant who has done this before, and a set of best practices from the industry. We just spent a lot of time and money executing fifteen RCM analyses to proactively go after what you're calling defects. Why are you trying to re-invent what we already have?" Vance asked.

"Look, I appreciate your view, Vance, but I'm still not convinced that we have everything in place that we need, and I'm not taking Steve off this initiative." James felt the need to tread lightly with Vance, but he felt it was important that he stick to his guns on this one. "If you'd like," James continued, "I can put him into the old reliability manager's role that has been vacant for some time, and you can backfill the position."

"Fine," Vance bit out, "if that's what you want to do. It just seems like a waste of talent. And while I'm on the topic of resources, Robert and I have been doing some work on getting to the next step. We figure that it's going to take two more planners and two more inspectors to get us over the hump, in addition to an extension with MRS to do ten more RCM studies."

"And how do you propose we pay for that?" James asked. "We're already way over budget."

"It's short term, James. When the plan is fully operational, it will more than pay for itself."

"Well, I don't know what your definition of short term is, but it's been six months, and costs have only gone one direction and that's up! We're going to have to resource this with current staffing."

"Okay, James, but you're the one that has to answer to Jennings. I'm just telling you what I think we need," with that, Vance stood up and left the office.

James groaned out loud in frustration after Vance had cleared the office door.

James decided to delve deeper into the request for more planners and inspectors. He got up out of his chair and stomped down to the room where Robert was sitting that day. "Robert, Vance tells me that you want us to hire two more planners and two more inspectors. Is that right?"

Robert slowly turned his chair around and faced James, "Yeah, I'm glad you came down to chat about that. I'm afraid that you're getting into a lot of trouble with Jennings, and I just want to help you out."

James felt his hackles rise at this response but contained himself. "So, let me get this straight. You think that a couple more planners and inspectors will save me from Jennings?"

Robert grabbed a three ring binder from the desk. Flipping to a number of pages of work order data, as well as the metrics on planned maintenance, he pushed it over for James to view as he pointed to a figure on the bottom of the page, "The results show that the percent of planned work that was completed on schedule is at 48%. The goal is to achieve 95% planned and scheduled work, so there needs to be a drastic improvement."

James again restrained himself and asked, "Exactly what is your definition of 95% planned and scheduled work, Robert?"

"The definition of planned and scheduled is that all of the material is ready, and the job is scheduled at least a week ahead of time. That way the operations people have plenty of lead time to take the equipment out of service and have it ready to go. This is what we need to avoid wasting the time of our most precious resource, maintenance time," Robert answered earnestly.

This comment really got under James' skin, and he quickly shot back, "So we should stop our production so the precious mechanics can get their work done? Is that it?"

Robert frowned and declared, "If the maintenance is not done, you won't produce any of your precious product, so they have to come first."

James took a deep breath and asked in a calmer voice, "How did you accomplish that when you were here ten years ago, Robert?"

Robert lit up, "We had a great operations manager back then, and he dictated that operations had to take the equipment down whenever maintenance requested it. That was an enlightened time around here."

James, recognizing the barb, asked, "How long did that last? Obviously less than ten years since we don't have that policy today?"

Robert smirked and replied, "It lasted until the operations manager left a couple years later. He was a really strong leader, like a 900 pound gorilla, and when he bellowed, everyone jumped."

"So that ops. manager got you to your goal of 95% planned and scheduled maintenance?"

Robert squirmed in his seat and replied, "Well, no, he wasn't here long enough to get it that far. But we made it to 80%, and he was pushing for more planners and inspectors when he was forced out."

James saw his opportunity and asked with a smile, "Why was he forced out?"

"Uhm, he got blamed for some missed shipments that really weren't his fault. I think those corporate guys resented him for having a high percent of planned maintenance. In fact, this is a common experience we have at MRS. We get a guy who really understands what we want him to do and he gets kicked out because of some production shortfall. But, it never fails that a few years later they come back to us and want to start over again because they're back down below 60% planned and scheduled work."

James smirked and replied, his voice dripping with sarcasm he could not hold back, "I guess that's good job security for you, at least."

Robert, apparently missing the sarcasm, replied, "Yeah, I guess that's the silver lining all right."

James was furious. But he clamped his mouth closed and stood up to leave. He excused himself by saying, "I have to go now, but I told Vance that he'll have to make these changes with the resources we have in place. We're too far over budget as it is."

James stalked back to his office, closed the door for privacy, and sat in his chair to calm down before he bit somebody's head off. He just couldn't wrap his head around it. He simply wanted to protect his employees and make the plant safe and profitable, but a handful of people were hell-bent on making his life miserable.

James finally had a break to call Chance later that afternoon. He was so frustrated with Vance and the discussion they'd had earlier, he felt the need to vent with Chance. After explaining the incident, James was surprised at Chance's calmness.

"Well, unfortunately, I think this situation is pretty typical. Your maintenance manager has got his goals and means mixed up. He thinks the goal is installing the planned maintenance approach when in reality it is just a tool. It sounds like he has a fair amount of his ego tied to it."

"Yeah," responded James, "I have a plant that is slipping back to reactive mode, a maintenance manager who is fighting to keep us headed toward planning, and I'm not even sure that if we're successful, I'm going to reach my manufacturing goals."

Chance let out what James thought of as his "I know something you don't know" chuckle.

"You know, it's really fascinating. I've been reading a fair amount lately, and I happened to stumble across some great stuff from DuPont Chemical Company. There's an article they put out based on worldwide benchmarking that describes reliability as a movement between stable domains. Each domain can be sustained for long periods of time, but it takes the right set of activities to get there. Can I take a minute and lay it out for you? I think it might be helpful. I'm faxing over a diagram now. They used it in the article. I'll wait while you go get it."

"Sure," said James, "hold on just a minute." James put Chance on hold and went to the fax machine just outside his office. Sure enough, it was in the process of receiving a fax.

James impatiently waited for the machine to finish receiving as he drummed his fingers on the counter. He looked up at Lorraine, seeing her questioning look, and winked at her. She sputtered at him and turned away as the machine finally finished spitting out his fax.

James chuckled to himself. His capable assistant was so formal. He got a huge kick out of throwing her off balance now and again. Still smiling, he grabbed the piece of paper, quickly walked back into his office, sat down at his desk, and picked up the phone again. James stabbed at the holding line, put the receiver up to his ear and stated, "Got it." He looked over the diagram Chance had sent.

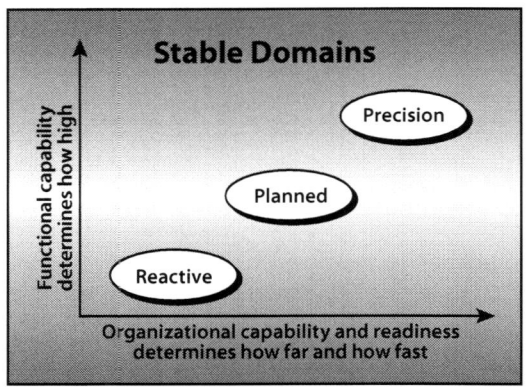

"Well, let me explain what you're looking at there. You'll notice that the first stable domain that they describe is the Reactive Domain. It's where most of the DuPont plants were in the benchmark. This domain does not mean that there is no planned work. It typically means that 40-50% of the work is reacting to failures. This domain is characterized by all of the issues that you've been facing: late deliveries, low capacity utilization, accidents, high cost to operate, "us" versus "them" mentality between maintenance and operations. Actually, since you're still only at 48% planned maintenance, you're still in that Reactive Domain."

James sat back in his chair and listened attentively, knowing Chance always made good points.

"The second domain they call the Planned Domain. It's really similar to where you're headed with MRS. The good news is that they saw significant improvement in plants in that domain just like the MRS data. Costs were lower and production better. However, what they found was that it took a very coordinated effort to move a plant out of the Reactive Domain and into the Planned. The Reactive Domain can be maintained without the same coordination because the equipment is constantly telling you what to do. In the Planned Domain, you have to make the calls. If you have different people pulling in different directions, you simply slip back to the Reactive Domain.

"In the model of the systems work we've been doing, you can think of reactive work as a very natural balancing feedback loop where the equipment tells you what to work on. Planned maintenance is a very unnatural balancing loop where you have to anticipate where the defects are and take action. I think that's what's happening to you now.

"The DuPont article also makes it clear that there is substantial additional work involved in the transition from reactive to planned as you have to do all of the new planned work and maintain most of the reactive work for some time. They indicate that this is where many of their efforts to get to the Planned Domain failed. They simply lacked the resources and the will to get all of the work done."

James tapped his pencil on the desk, deep in concentration, while everything Chance had explained sank in. "You know, that's really interesting. That's exactly how it feels right now. We have an uncoordinated effort, and it feels like we're slipping back into the Reactive Domain. It certainly feels like we're putting out a lot more effort for the same results," James added.

Chance chuckled and replied, "The third domain apparently surprised the DuPont folks. They called it the Precision Domain. They really thought that excellent planning was the top of the performance ladder. However, they found much higher performance in some Japanese plants. These plants were very different. While they also did much of their work in a planned way, what was striking was their focus on eliminating the causes of their issues, instead of the symptoms. The Japanese called it Total Productive Maintenance, or TPM, which I've heard of but really don't know much about. However, the principles are strikingly similar to the approach we used at St. Louis.

"Operator PMs and cleaning are a big part of it. They have a systematic way of going after design defects and putting preventive plans in place. What's really unique is their approach to defect elimination. They go after individual defects in small team activities. What is astounding is the level of performance improvement that they're reporting in the benchmarks. Literally 80-90% of the failures have disappeared in the Precision Domain. It reminded me of the 'half defect' scenario that Mark, the professor from MIT, showed us. Costs are significantly less than either of the other domains, and production is up and more reliable. I really think there is something here that you can use."

"I have to admit it does feel like the road map I've been looking for. It describes our current situation pretty well and the struggles we're having with the MRS system. You send me the materials on the small team activity, and I'll get Steve and Reese to pilot it on the Extrusion line," James stated firmly, his mind made up.

"Sure, and I'm also going to send you a gem of a book that I used in St. Louis, by Robert Schaffer, called *The Breakthrough Strategy*. It's perfect for putting together small teams. In the meantime, I'll look deeper into this DuPont work and TPM to see if there is anything else we can use."

"A book?" James exclaimed. "Do you really think with all that I've got going on that I have time to read a book?"

"Relax," Chance assured him, chuckling, "it's very short. You can read it and get the gist of the approach in an hour or so. Trust me, you need the help," Chance admonished.

"Okay, okay, I'll look for it in the mail. Thanks, I'll talk to you soon."

James hung up the phone and clasped his hands behind his head in thought. A book was not what he needed right now, but Chance always had his finger on the pulse of things. He'd make time to read the damn book he decided as he looked at his watch, pushed back from his desk, and exited his office to do some final rounds and check in with a few folks before considering heading home for the day.

The book, *The Breakthrough Strategy*, arrived the next day. As Chance had promised, it was short and to the point. James read the entire book that evening before going to bed, and he had to admit it was enlightening.

The author, Robert Schaffer, had a simple premise: organizations accomplish extraordinary things when there is a crisis like a natural disaster, strike, or emergency order. His book examined the causes of this lift in performance and how to harness it without the crisis. James thought the key boiled down to just a couple of simple concepts. Shaffer found that people perform their best when there is:

- A sense of urgency and challenge
- A definition of success that is near and clear
- A need for people to collaborate
- A fear of failure
- An exciting and novel approach
- An opportunity for people to experiment

James had specifically noted that Shaffer believed these conditions could be reproduced in small projects that over time could change the performance of an organization and, at the same time, change the culture. The key was launching small Breakthrough Projects that Shaffer defined as:

"A planned project that is urgent and compelling, has a bottom-line goal that is achievable in a short period of time (weeks), the participants feel ready, willing and able to accomplish, and can be achieved with available resources and authority."

James thought the approach was brilliant for defect elimination. If they could get small teams of people to eliminate defects and sources of defects, they could replicate the performance that Shaffer described in his book.

The key points would be for the teams to be cross-functional so that all the required skills would be represented and that they picked a defect not only important to the plant but also one that the team was passionate about. James was not going to put a manager or engineer on each team to facilitate. He simply could not spare the time. The team members were going to have to complete the project on their own. This would require they have some personal passion to get it done. The team would have to work within its current authority and resources. If he ignored that aspect, all of the supervisors and functional managers would have his head. Finally, the teams would not have the authority to recommend someone else eliminate the defect. They would have to eliminate the defects themselves. If this turned into a laundry list of things that supervisors needed to do, or worse yet, a list of things he needed to do, it would go nowhere. It was clear these could not be "suggestion" teams; they needed to be "action" teams.

Over the next few weeks, James and his shadow network worked to get the operator PM program moved to another line in the plant. They also started doing small team activities on the Extrusion line using the principles from *The Breakthrough Strategy*. Since they had not yet completed the forensic defect study to determine which defects were the most important, Reese had come up with the idea of working on the defects associated with their current failures.

The Extrusion line had come up with the slogan, "Don't Just Fix It… Improve It." They treated every failure in the area as an opportunity to remove the defects that caused it. Each team was a mix of operators and mechanics, and an occasional engineer when required.

Steve and Reese met with every team at the kick-off and emphasized the need to eliminate defects at their source. They also made it clear that hierarchy was not a factor on the teams. Everyone's ideas counted and everyone was expected to contribute and take action.

Within a few short weeks, everyone on the Extrusion line had participated in at least one defect elimination team, and many had participated in more than one. Reese had started giving out stickers for every team that wiped out a defect, and the teams had taken to wearing them on their hard hats like college football players do on their helmets. The shadow network had debated whether recognition should go to everyone who participated on a defect elimination team or just the individual who completed the action. After all, many of the defects were really small and participation varied. In the end, Reese prevailed with his argument that no matter the size of the defect, everyone who participates in an action team should be recognized.

However, as happy as James was with the improvements that had been made in some areas, he was extremely disappointed on the planned side. Things were still pretty rocky. Vance's relationship with Buzz and the whole operations team was starting to deteriorate badly. There was a power struggle going on, and Vance was determined to get his way. It was not uncommon to hear them going at it first thing in the morning as they discussed the production schedule. Vance was now convinced that Buzz was deliberately sabotaging the planned effort, and Buzz was getting more and more defensive. Vance was in James' office almost daily now, either complaining about cooperation in the plant or requesting more resources.

The CMMS was a particular issue. The data loading was continuing to be a huge time sink. It was clear that as the plant was falling back into more reactive work, and as Vance continued pushing inspections and planning, there was simply no time left to do a proper job getting the system up. The "go live" date was only a few weeks away, and no one had addressed it, but they were either going to have to put in a system with major holes in it, or they were going to miss that deadline.

Vance had also decided that the focus on defect elimination by James, and the folks in his network, was getting in the way of the planned maintenance program. Since James was clearly the champion, Vance did not come out against it directly, but behind the scenes he was making it hard for the maintenance people to participate and constantly challenging the work they were doing. James considered confronting him on the issue but did not have anything concrete to discuss since all of the resistance was passive and behind the scenes.

James knew that it would take everyone in the plant to work on defects, not just the maintenance manager. He worked tirelessly over the next few weeks knowing that defects were a constant problem. He worked on getting his employees 100% on board, while promoting defect elimination. He knew that Corporate had their own agenda and that defect elimination was not even close to the top of their list, which made things difficult. He often felt like he was walking a tight rope as he tried to accommodate corporate initiatives while working on his plan to create a network of his own to accomplish his goals.

A Long, Lonely Road of Trials

It had been nine months since the planned initiative began with MRS. James called together a meeting of his direct reports, along with Robert from MRS, to try and re-align the team. He decided to have the meeting off-site for two days in the North Georgia Mountains. He was hoping a little team building might help, given the tensions.

James approved the agenda that had been prepared by Robert. The first day consisted of a half day of team building activities and a half day of implementation review followed by a dinner outing that included bowling. The second day was divided up between the three major thrusts of the plan, PM and PdM, Proactive RCM's, and the CMMS. James had added an intentionally vague topic at the end called "Other Activities" where he intended to discuss some of the successes of the shadow network and see if he could get the formal network to get behind some of the efforts.

As dawn broke on the first day of the team building meeting, James was optimistic and looking forward to building more camaraderie at his site.

The team building consultant, that Robert had recommended, led them through the usual activities, including racing to see which team could get all its members across a lava field, and having one team member fall back, while trusting the other team members to catch them. It had all felt a little hokey to James, but he had to admit that it seemed to work.

Vance and Buzz were smiling and laughing with each other and seemed to remember for the first time in months that they were on the same team. They actually seemed to enjoy each other's company. Robert was also getting into the mix with everyone and becoming part of the team. James was all smiles as they broke for lunch, thinking to himself that maybe this session would pay off after all.

After lunch, the tide turned when they buckled down to review the progress the site had made. Unfortunately, the fireworks and recriminations started almost immediately. As they reviewed the progress over the last month, it was clear that there was not much positive to report. PM and PdM compliance was at its lowest point since the first month of the project. Naturally, both Buzz and Vance blamed each other for this predicament.

Atlanta Scorecard 4: July 1st			
Key Performance Indicator	Description	Atlanta Plant Current Year Forecast	Best in Class
Maintenance as a % of Replacement Value	Maintenance cost, excluding capital compared to the estimated capital cost to replace the plant equipment	4.0%	2%
Overtime %	Percent of overtime for hourly workers	29%	<5%
Waste cost as a percent of raw materials cost	The cost of all scrap and defective output compared to total input	2.1%	0.2%
Raw material cost per ton of output	Applied only to plants making similar outputs	$18.71	$20
Labor cost per ton of output	Applied only to plants making similar outputs	$13.07	$7.30
Consumables, parts and outside repairs cost per ton		$5.97	$2.50
Energy costs per ton		$7.65	$7.25
% Planned Maintenance Work	% of work that is planned and scheduled at least 1 week in advance	68%	95%
Production % of Max	Maximum production the plant can operate at	81%	98%
Earnings	Last 12 months earnings in millions of dollars	$4.1 million (loss)	$40 million (profit)
Recordable injuries/ 200K man hours		2.77	<0.50

"You guys in maintenance seem to always know the absolute worst time to ask for equipment to be shut down, and we've documented a slew of times that there wasn't anything wrong with the equipment but you requested we bring it down. We waste all of that production time for nothing!" Buzz stated heatedly. "Based on James' input, I've continued to put production over maintenance scheduling, but the last time I looked, our customers weren't paying us to maintain the equipment. They're paying us for product."

Vance couldn't help but take the bait. As he sat up straighter in his chair with a gleam in his eye, he said, "Well then, it seems that based on this strategy, we should be setting new production records. Uhm… let's just scan down the line on our reports and see how we're doing." Vance feigned a good imitation of a completely surprised, over-acting stage performer and covered his mouth in surprise, "Wow! Shocking! We're running almost exactly the same as when this project started. No throughput improvement." Vance sat back with a smug expression and crossed his arms over his chest, "Seems to blow your theory right out of the water, huh, Buzz?"

Robert, trying to calm the escalating tensions, interjected before Buzz could respond, "Now, guys, it is true that performance is not where we want it to be or where it needs to be, but we *have* made tremendous progress. We have over eight thousand PM jobs in the system, and we've completed nearly twenty RCM's. We've got ten inspectors out in the plant every day finding abnormal operating conditions. On top of that, we're just days away from launching a state of the art CMMS. That's a lot of change to absorb, and you just can't expect everything to be running perfectly smooth."

When Robert recapped it in that way, it did seem like a lot of progress, but James knew better. No one at Corporate was going to give them credit for their actions. He knew they wanted results, and they wanted them yesterday.

The team spent the rest of the afternoon arguing over why planned jobs were not getting done, whether they were really ready to cut over to the new CMMS, and why so few of the RCM recommendations had been accomplished, months after the recommendations. They also argued about a host of other issues in which very little was resolved. They spent a great deal of time rehashing long held animosities while defending their own positions. As the meeting broke up, Robert and James were alone in the meeting room reflecting on the day's progress.

"Well, I thought this morning went really well, at least. The team building seemed to be just what the doctor ordered," Robert stated optimistically.

James replied with a dejected shrug, "Yeah, I guess so. But it really made no difference in this afternoon's session. You know, I've come to believe that we focus too much on the first word in teamwork and not enough on the second," James said as he slumped in his chair in frustration.

"How do you mean?" asked Robert.

"Well," James replied, "we've always been a pretty good team. We all get along, you know. We like each other and everything. You saw that today. Send us into a softball league, and we would have a ball. It's not the team thing we struggle with…it's the work. The work we're doing pits us against each other. If we don't find some way to change the nature of the work, I'm just not sure this team is going to make it," James stated emphatically as he closed his notebook.

Dinner that evening was a somber affair and many decided to skip the bowling event that had been planned in order to catch up on the e-mails they had all missed that day.

Having just cleared out his own e-mail in-box, James tried to wind down as he sat up in bed contemplating the day's events. All the comments that had been made that day kept running through his head. He was frustrated by all the arguing and posturing going on, but he simply did not know how to change it. The e-mail he received from Jennings that day was weighing heavily on his mind. He worked late into the night trying to find a solution. He fell asleep sitting up in bed with his files in his lap.

The next morning James started off the session by reading the e-mail he had received the day before from Jennings.

To: All Plant Managers
From: Marshall Jennings

RE: Cost reduction initiative

In preparation for the upcoming meeting with Wall Street analysts, our CEO has announced a major cost reduction initiative to boost earnings. To accomplish our goals there will be cuts throughout the organization including Sales, Marketing, Corporate Overhead and Manufacturing. Our piece in manufacturing will be to cut all costs, excluding raw materials, by 20% over the next 12 months. While this will not be easy or painless, I am sure you all understand that growing earnings is essential to providing value to our shareholders and that you will whole heartedly join me in supporting this initiative.

There is a five step cost reduction approach that we will be undertaking attached to this e-mail. A facilitator from Corporate will be assigned to each plant and will assist in executing this plan. I will be having a kick-off meeting on this initiative next Thursday and expect all of you to attend with an initial plan for the proposed cuts at your plant.

Everyone sat frozen in silence for a moment, as the contents of the memo and its ramifications sank in. They all knew that a 20% reduction was going to be extremely tough. Honestly, James thought they'd be lucky to get back to flat with last year's cost.

Discussion finally erupted amongst the meeting attendees. They quickly decided to scrap the rest of the agenda for the day and focus on the five-step plan that James had printed out and copied for each person at the meeting. It was completely deflating. The steps were generic enough:

1. Put your costs in ratios that can be compared across sites.
2. Benchmark your costs against your sister plants and our "best practice" measures. Determine which costs need improvement.
3. Define the drivers of each cost to be improved.
4. Create a plan to attack each of the drivers over the next 3 weeks.
5. Track and report progress on the drivers.

There were a number of mandatory and recommended cost ratios given in a table in the attachment, along with the best practice numbers. Wayne Darby, the plant comptroller, was busy pulling together as many of the numbers as he could by working his cell phone with his staff back at the plant. As Wayne assembled the plant's results in one column and the best practice in another, the true size of the challenge became apparent to all.

James combed his hand through his hair in frustration. It was worse than he'd expected. With the exception of raw materials cost, they were not even close to the benchmark. Next Thursday was going to be ugly.

Wayne looked at the numbers and shook his head solemnly.

"What's on your mind, Wayne?" James asked.

"Well, it's really a shame. You know, seven years ago we had maintenance costs down to about 1% of replacement value. That was the last time I benchmarked these numbers. If we could have only held that performance…." Wayne's statement drifted off as he continued to go over the numbers.

James looked at Wayne with a puzzled expression. He'd also been at the plant seven years ago, and he didn't have very fond memories of that time. The plant manager at the time was a real jerk who didn't' give a flip about people. As far as James was concerned, he'd single-handedly run the plant into the ground and had been lucky enough to get promoted out before the plant went through a string of critical failures. If that's what it took to get to world class - no, thank you, James thought to himself.

The team spent some time brainstorming cost drivers and gave a halfhearted effort to come up with a game plan to attack them. They completely lost steam by 4:00 pm and decided to call it a day.

As everyone was filing out of the meeting room, Robert pulled James aside, "I'm going to talk to Jennings and see if we can get Atlanta some relief on this initiative. We've come too far on the planned initiative to go backwards now. I'm sure I can convince him to give you some room."

"Thanks," James responded but without much hope.

After dinner that night, James called Chance to go over the day's news.

Before the preliminaries were even over, Chance started right in, "I bet I can guess what you're calling about. Before you attack me, just realize this was also news to me. Although, I can take some blame for those benchmarks since many of them come from my old buddies in the St Louis plant. I have to give them credit, they've not only continued, but they've surpassed my performance there."

"I have to be honest, Chance, I'm not sure I can do it. This cost cutting initiative on top of the planned initiative, which, by the way, is driving costs up. My people are maxed out. If I throw one more initiative at them, they're going to revolt. And if I have to spend anymore additional time at the plant, I am going to need a good divorce lawyer."

"I understand," Chance replied. "This is a classic case of initiative overload from Corporate. We can't manage to get any one thing done because we're too busy trying to get ten done. I can tell you one thing from experience, James, but you're not going to like it. I haven't seen your numbers yet, but the other reports you've shared with me give me a pretty good indication of where you stand. You can't achieve the goals set out in that announcement today following the approach given. You're going to have to decide whether you're going to pursue the results, or the process, because you can't do both."

"I know. You're absolutely right, Chance," James replied with a chuckle, "I don't like it at all!" They both laughed out loud.

"You know," James continued, "I found out today that our plant was actually at the maintenance cost benchmark seven years ago. My controller was lamenting that we didn't hold it there," James added.

"Unfortunately, that's a very backwards way of looking at it. I know the history of that plant well. The only way Atlanta ever got close to the maintenance benchmark was when that boob stopped repairing things. Anyone can get costs down that way for a while, but remember, defects age. You can leave them alone for a while, and the results are not that bad, but, eventually, they will come back, only bigger in size and consequences. I just saw an article by the DuPont guys, and they describe that exact scenario, calling it the Regressive Domain. When you treat a consequence, such as cost, like a goal, there are a number of ways to achieve it that are absolutely counter to the true business goals," Chance replied.

"You know, I had a similar thought when he said it, but not as clearly as you just stated it. I have to say, it's tempting to just give them what they ask for."

"I hear you, but remember Todd and his eye? That accident was the call to change, you know, like in the Hero's Journey. It's what started all of this, and you need to remember how you felt right after the accident. Don't forget all of the folks there who are counting on you to do the right thing.

James grimaced and replied, "I know, I know."

"Don't forget, this is our road of trials. We were expecting there to be problems to work through. It's the normal way of things, so don't give up now. You're just going to have to work through all of these issues to successfully complete the journey."

"You're right, Chance. I'll keep plugging away."

"Good. So, are we still on for tomorrow afternoon with the shadow network?" Chance asked. "If so, send me your cost figures and the numbers underlying them first thing in the morning. We'll add that topic to the agenda. Look, the good news is that the benchmarks show that you can easily meet the cost targets if you can get the site to do the right things."

James agreed. "Yeah, we're on. I'll talk to you tomorrow. And thanks for your help, Chance."

"You bet. Bye."

The following day back at the office, James was cleaning up some last minute details before the 4th of July weekend.

Robert showed up at the entrance to his office and leaned against the door jam, "Well buddy, I gave Jennings my best pitch but no dice. Atlanta is going to have to make its numbers like all the rest. Sorry!" Robert said with a grimace.

James shook his head in frustration and dropped his pen on the desk. He was not surprised. In fact, it was exactly the answer he'd expected.

The day passed quickly as James attended to a string of administrative tasks that had been neglected because of the two days he'd been off-site. He spent some time with various direct reports re-validating the numbers for Thursday and working with them on preliminary plans. Despite what Chance said the night before, he could not show up without something prepared.

When six-thirty rolled around, James shuffled into the conference room with the rest of the shadow network, and they placed the call to Chance. There was a lot to cover, but James' heart just wasn't in it. He could not help but think that the shadow network was a luxury he could no longer afford. It had been an interesting idea, and he'd gathered a great group of folks, but how could he keep it up with two huge corporate initiatives to execute?

Cindy, the plant engineer, was leading the meeting and ticking through the agenda. "We'll start with a recap of the planned program - PMs, PdMs, RCMs and the CMMS. Then we'll get an update from Steve on the forensic defect analysis. Then Reese will update us on the action teams on the Extrusion line and the operator PM program. Finally, I think James and Chance want to talk about the Cost Initiative for a minute. Did I miss anything?" Cindy asked with a searching glance at everyone gathered around the table.

No one spoke up sc Cindy continued jumping right into the planned initiative recap.

James had heard it all before, more bickering between maintenance and operations, more inspections, more planning, more PMs in the system but very limited results. And to top it all off, costs were out of control. More RCMs had been done, and everyone seemed to agree that each analysis was the product of a lot of hard work and intelligent problem solving. The issue was that the performance of the equipment that had been RCM'd was not much better than before. Of course, this was no fault of the analysis, Cindy pointed out. It was really a failure of execution, and by definition, someone else's problem.

Steve was up next and started in on the forensic analysis. "Well, I have to say this was a fascinating exercise. Let me skip to the bottom line." He put up a slide of the defect source breakdown the team had found. "What we found is that our sources of defects are highly weighted to operating practices, maintenance workmanship, parts quality, and to a lesser extent, design. Notice that wear is a distant sixth. We didn't include aging as a source since it was too hard to pull out of the data. This confirmed Chance's point," Steve concluded. "We have a clear picture of the enemy now. Anyone want to see it?" Steve asked playfully. He held up a large picture of the entire plant operating team that had been taken at the last all-site picnic. The room erupted into laughter.

Chance waited for the laughter to die down before commenting, "If you think about it, it's really great news. It says that over 70% of the defects are in your control. I can't wait to see what impact this has on the simulation model. So far they have just made guesses at the defect rates in the model." He added enthusiastically, "I thought it would be high, but I never guessed that high. It also agrees with some outside data on failure curves that I stumbled onto from RCM analysis and Navy studies."

Chance asked Cindy to pass around copies of the graphic that he had faxed to her earlier. The title was, "Failure Patterns", and the figures were based on the RCM studies.

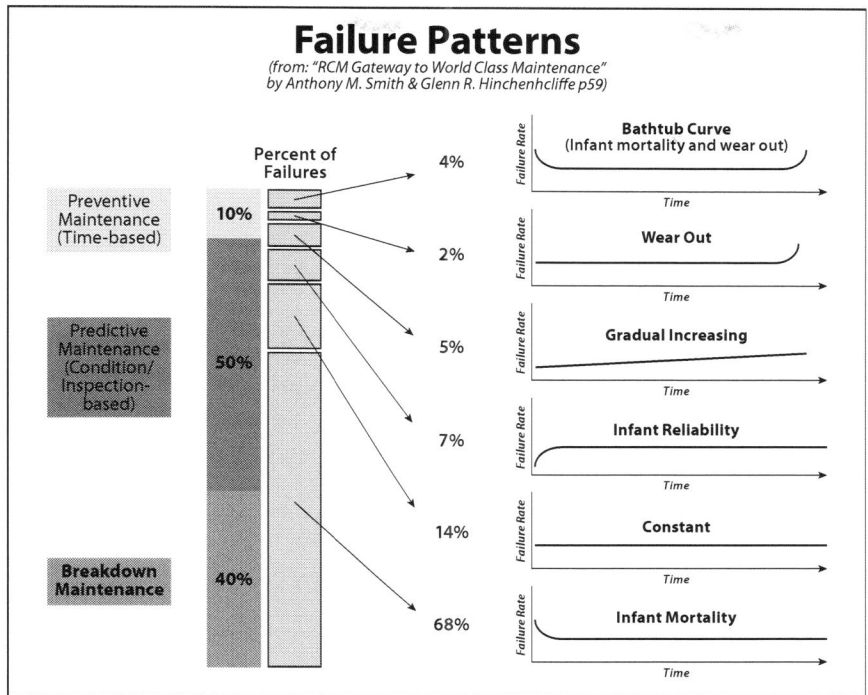

As Cindy passed out copies, Chance continued, "As everybody receives their copy, I'll explain it. Basically, it shows a similar pattern. Almost 70% of failures fall into the 'random failure mode.' Every place in the failure patterns handout where the line is flat and horizontal represents random failures. That typically means that some operator, design, part, or workmanship defect got into the equipment and caused a failure long before wear or aging could have an effect. So, just like your study, around 70% of the defects are due to actions of people in the organization.

"What's more, the authors of one study showed the link between types of maintenance. With so many random failures, you simply can't get planned work to be more than 50-60% of total work without the operation being shut down all of the time. The nature of the incoming defects makes it impossible to get into a highly planned routine. The system really creates the behavior."

James had been looking forward to the results of this analysis for the last six weeks, and he had to admit the results were somewhat shocking. He was having trouble, however, thinking about the implications with so many other priorities on his mind. The team continued discussing the methodology, as well as some of the pitfalls and smaller learnings.

When it was time to transition, Reese perked up and was nothing short of giddy as he stood up and began, "Well, we've had a ton of teams structured off of the *Breakthrough Strategy*. Each team has worked a defect. In all, we have had thirty teams in the last two months. Now, most have tackled really small things that, to be honest, I would have a tough time quantifying.

"For example, the extractor team worked on a failure we had with the #2 extractor. They discovered that the inner O-ring was missing and that the installation instructions were incorrect. They fixed both. Each time that extractor fails, it costs $150-$300 to repair and it's failed three times this year.

"The steam team decided to find and eliminate all steam leaks in the line. They found over fifty. They estimate that the savings will be $400-$500 a month in energy costs, not to mention the safety issues involved. But the most exciting example was one that just wrapped up yesterday. As you know, we have had a rash of failures on the main drive motor of the line. In a previous meeting, we talked about a vibration that was ignored and how it led to a failure that bent the drive shaft. Well, it was repaired, but as usual, no effort was made to find the root cause.

"One of the teams decided that was unacceptable and took it on as a project. They eventually found that the tolerance on the bearings was incorrect. Apparently, an inexperienced stores person thought that a tighter tolerance meant a better bearing and started ordering the wrong one. Well, every time it had been replaced in the last five years, the old one was replaced with the exact same bearing. It cost literally nothing to fix this defect, and we have spent well over ten thousand dollars in repairs on that motor in the last twelve months, not to mention the lost production."

"That's fantastic news," James chimed in. "How is it we've gotten traction so quickly on this versus the RCM work? I don't want to sound disparaging, but the way we've picked defects has been a little haphazard compared to the rigor of RCM, and yet we have all of these results."

Cindy sat up and interjected, "I think I can shed some light on that. When I first started hearing about some of the successes from Reese, I was skeptical. Since I'd participated on several of the RCMs, I wanted to see for myself what the differences were, so I decided to join a team, and you're right, James, that the rigor is not even close. I was actually a little embarrassed by how simple the diagnosis and solutions were on my team. However, I can tell you that the focus is very different. The action team lived up to its name. We were completely focused on taking action. The second major difference was the buy in. The operators and the mechanics on my team were totally committed to finding a solution and getting it implemented. That felt very different than the RCM team where the facilitator and engineer seemed dedicated to completing the analysis, but the rest of the folks seemed to feel their role was just to be there to answer questions.

"The other stunning thing to me was the level of detailed knowledge the operators had. I found that I, as well as the other engineers, knew better than anyone how the equipment was supposed to run, but the operators knew the reality of how it really ran. There are so many workarounds and irregular operations that only these front-line guys can give you the real picture of where the defects are, and how they can be eliminated.

"I guess I would have to say that the whole thing was a bit contagious. Once you see how many small defects there are, and how simple it is to knock one out, it is hard not to want to take on another. In fact, after my first team experience, I went back and pulled one of the failure modes from one of the RCMs that I had participated in and sponsored a team of my own. Do you know we eliminated that failure mode in one afternoon? I think there could be a link between the RCMs and these action teams. The failure modes are an excellent source of defects to tackle."

James could feel the team's energy rising as everyone listened to Cindy intently, and he was getting a little fired up himself. Finally some positive momentum, he thought.

"I have to agree with everything Cindy has said," Reese interjected. "My only challenge is communicating to folks why we need them to do this, what it will do for them and the plant, and what we expect of them. Once they do it, as Cindy says, it becomes somewhat contagious, but getting people to a point of understanding, and getting them interested in the beginning, is a real challenge. I've been able to muscle these first few through with a lot of personal attention and arm twisting, but that's not sustainable long term."

Reese then went on to recap the results of the operator PMs and concluded by showing the results of the Extrusion line. James could hardly believe what he was seeing. The Extrusion line had improved on almost every measure in just four months. Uptime and throughput were up, emergency call-outs, overtime, maintenance costs, waste and energy costs were all down. Even the planned numbers were up. James asked if Robert and the MRS team were doing anything different in the area, but the answer came back negative. Something seemed fishy to James, but he couldn't quite put his finger on it. How could the planned maintenance initiative, that was struggling everywhere else, be doing so well in the extruder line?

Chance interrupted James' thoughts, "Well, are we ready to discuss the cost initiative?"

"Sure," said James.

"As I reviewed your numbers, I had two thoughts. First, anytime you look at costs that are too high, you should ask yourself whether you have expenses per activity that are too high, or the wrong amount or type of activities. If the expenses per activity are too high, this is a procurement and negotiation issue. If, however, the nature or amount of activity is wrong, then you have a work issue. As I look at your numbers, it's very clear yours is a work issue not a procurement issue. You seem to be buying and paying the right amounts but on too much work. The second observation I made is your cost ratios per ton. You have more of a denominator problem than a numerator problem. There are certainly opportunities to take cost down but there are even greater opportunities to spread the costs over more production," Chance concluded.

"Interesting, I don't think that I would have looked at it in quite that way. I'll make sure to incorporate it into my plans for Thursday," James replied thoughtfully.

"On the model front, I don't have such good news," Chance admitted as they shifted gears. "I had the opportunity, a couple of weeks ago, to take some of the leaders from other plants through the work we've done. What a snore fest I'm here to tell you. I showed them the basics behind the model and the results of various scenarios. They could not have been less interested. It was such a contrast to the sessions that we've had in the development process. It seems that the model is not as good a tool for communicating and training as I had hoped."

"You know what was different?" Cindy observed. "The model was interesting to us because we were creating it. It forced us to question how things really worked, how decisions were made, and the impact of those decisions. I can see where just a presentation of that same material would be pretty dry."

"Yeah, the act of creating the model was very different. It was more like the Beer Distribution Game, where you experience the dynamics and deal with them. That's what we really need, a game that reinforces how important defect elimination is. It should illustrate what we've learned while allowing people to experience it and discover the answer for themselves," James said, voicing his thoughts out loud.

"That's an interesting concept," Chance answered. "That could help with both my problem and Reese's. We could use a game to train new managers on the approach, but also use it as a tool to give the early action teams a virtual experience in making the transition that we're trying to create for the real plant."

The team seemed very enthusiastic about the concept, and Chance promised to follow up with the MIT team.

They wrapped up the meeting after setting a time to meet the following month. They set up a tentative agenda, and James hoped he would not be announcing the end of the network in that meeting.

James headed home late that night, looking forward to having the following day off for the 4th of July. Carol had planned a huge family barbeque, and he was looking forward to a little downtime.

James went back to work on Friday to a skeleton crew, a large part of his staff opting to use one of their floating holidays. He dealt with the normal issues at the plant as well as preparations for next Thursday's kick-off meeting. At the end of the day, James sent his numbers up to Jennings as requested.

The following Wednesday night, James boarded the plane at Atlanta's Hartsfield Airport to attend the managers' meeting at Corporate. He felt ready for the meeting because he had done all of the prep work requested but felt completely naked on the fundamental question of how he was going to make this latest initiative work with all of the other things going on.

James arrived at headquarters and headed for the conference room. It immediately became apparent that there was assigned seating. The tables were laid out facing the front of the room, with three chairs behind each table and a name placard at each seat. Looking around the room at the names, James quickly realized the rationale for the assigned seating. Jennings had placed each of the plant managers in the room, front to back, based on performance. His shoulders slumped a bit when he found his name in the back of the room next to the plant managers from Houston and Philadelphia. The manager from St. Louis was, of course, up in the front. James quickly moved to his seat.

Jennings started the meeting by recapping his e-mail and the rationale behind it. He emphasized the need to meet shareholder expectations.

He then put up a series of charts with each of the measures that James and the others had been collecting. It was misery, pure torture, as James squirmed in his chair in the back of the room. Chart after chart, James saw Atlanta near the bottom. In fact, Jennings singled him out on the maintenance cost chart as he stated, "And, James, back there has managed his second to last place position while piloting our planned maintenance initiative."

The morning session wrapped up with Jennings pushing them to "reach to the next level of performance".

James ducked out to grab lunch with Chance. Chance had been

working with the MIT team non-stop to turn the simulation into an interactive game for the Atlanta plant to use. He was very enthusiastic and thought they were heading in the right direction.

After lunch, James slunk back into the conference room and sat back down in his chair. Jennings began the afternoon with a series of small group activities focused on each of the measures, and plans to cut costs in those areas. Each manager selected which three they wanted to attend. During these sessions, Jennings had scheduled a one-on-one meeting with each of them to go over their plans.

James sat through two of the round tables but got very little out of them. Most of the managers only talked about things they would stop doing. In most cases, it sounded to James like robbing Peter to pay Paul. He couldn't help but think of Chance's reference to the Regressive Domain. The meeting felt like the expressway to the regressive mode.

During the third session, James found himself in the room with Drew, the plant manager in St. Louis. During the session there was the normal litany of things that would be forgone to meet the targets. But when it was Drew's turn to talk, he had a very different message.

"Well, to be honest, our performance on maintenance cost has really hit a plateau. We haven't seen any real improvement in almost a year. It became clear to me in preparing for this session that we have to find the next set of problems that are holding us back. 80% of our maintenance cost is associated with three issues: rotating equipment failures, electronic failures, and metallurgy.

"We took our rotating equipment from an average of eight months between failures to almost twenty-four months, but based on analysis my engineers have done, I see no reason we can't get to thirty-six months and beyond. We'll breakdown everything we're doing, including the designs of key equipment, and work to eliminate every source of failure.

"We are having too many failures at start-up on electrical. That indicates to me that we have parts issues and/or mechanical skill issues. We'll work on both.

"Finally, on metallurgy, we'll look at redesign on several components to eliminate corrosion and wear but realistically, like the rest of you, we're limited on capital investment. I'm also working with the local university on some corrosion inhibiting additives that could help."

James looked at him slack-jawed. Not a single cut offered for an important program. All of the focus was on improving reliability.

Billy Heard, the Houston plant manager, asked the question James wanted to know, "Right, but what are your cost cutting measures, Drew?

What you're saying sounds great but I don't see how it'll help you hit your goals. Don't you need some headcount reduction and parts stores reduction?"

"Well," James couldn't help but think Drew said smugly, "as I said, 80% of our maintenance is in these three areas. Our target is to eliminate roughly 30% of this work. The cost will come out of the parts that won't be used, the outside maintenance labor, which at our plant is nearly 30% of the total, and further attrition of our maintenance force. We've had a program of cross training mechanics on operations for some time now, and we've used the freed up resources to cover our attrition," Drew replied.

Before James could ask any questions of his own, Jennings' assistant tapped him on the shoulder and motioned that it was time for his one-on-one with the boss.

James saved his questions for later and made his way to Jennings' office taking the seat across from his desk. Jennings was tapping away on his keyboard, apparently still wrapping up an e-mail as James sat down. Jennings looked up, put away a file and opened another. As he looked down at it, he let out a sigh.

"Well, James," Jennings began, "Atlanta is certainly down in the bottom of the pack. I have to say, we made quite a commitment there giving you first crack at the planned maintenance initiative. I am more than a little disappointed. Now I have plant managers who are telling me, based on your results, that they don't want the initiative in their plant. Let's get down to it. How are you going to turn things around?"

James spent the next fifteen minutes going through the materials that he and the team had prepared. It was a litany of cuts to programs, deferral of "unnecessary" expenses, and positions to eliminate. All the while, he couldn't help but think of the plan he had just heard from Drew, the St. Louis plant manager.

Jennings stopped him when James came to cuts in the planned maintenance program. James had been careful to spin it as savings from wrapping up completed items, but Jennings was still unsure. There would be no more RCMs with outside facilitators. They would delay the CMMS implementation by three months, and one inspector and two planners would have to go.

At the end of his presentation, Jennings commented, "James, it seems like a reasonable plan. Do you feel confident it'll get you to the goal?"

"Yes," James lied, not really sure at all. It might get Jennings to his cost goal, but it would do almost nothing to help James get to his goals for the plant.

Jennings fired off a few more questions about the specifics of the plan, and then closing his folder and leaning back in his chair said, "James, I'm sure you understand that this time next year, I can't have Atlanta at the bottom of the heap. You've got to make this plan work."

James nodded and got up to leave. He walked to the door as if he were walking to a funeral. He had just explained and committed to a plan he was almost sure wouldn't help him reach his goals. As he grasped the door handle he turned back to Jennings.

"You know, you said something to me when you were in Atlanta last year right after the accident. You said that it was my plant and my decision on how to run things. I got the message that what you really care about are the results. Is that what you meant?"

"Sure, James," replied Jennings, completely unaware of the thoughts racing around in James' head. "I trust each of you to make your own decisions, but I expect results, and you can bet that I'll hold you accountable to those results. If you haven't noticed, I've stayed out of the way on this planned maintenance initiative. I've left it to you to shape and lead. I am not asking for any specific progress reports on this cost cutting initiative for three months, so I can give each of you some leeway in how you attack it. But make no mistake, I expect results."

The conversation was clearly over. James nodded and walked through the door. Although he felt a measure of freedom in what Jennings had just granted him, he wasn't quite sure what to do with that small measure of freedom. Just like Dorothy lamenting that she and her friends would never reach the Wizard after the flying monkeys stole Toto, forcing them to leave the yellow brick road to rescue him, he felt like he would never reach his destination on his own long and lonely road of trials.

Who's in Control?

The trip back to Atlanta was uneventful. James used the time on the plane alternatively thinking through the implementation of the plan he had shared with Jennings and thinking through ways to scrap the plan and try something else. He knew this much, when he got back he was going to have to bury himself in coming up with a solution. He had to get the situation under control.

James arrived home a little after nine o'clock in the evening. The kids were already in bed, and Carol was up watching TV. He had already practiced his, "Honey, I'm going to be busy," speech to her in the car. He started with an apology for having to check out for a few days and promised to make it up to her. He was just launching into all the things he promised to get done next month when Carol held up her hand and stopped him.

"That's all well and good, James," Carol said in an exasperated tone, "but did you forget the canoe trip with Susan that starts tomorrow? You promised to be a chaperone."

"What! That's this weekend?" James bellowed.

Carol rolled her eyes and pinned James with a glare, "Don't pretend you don't remember our discussion before you left for your meeting, James. You know darn well it's this weekend."

James got a sinking feeling. Susan was their oldest child and loved her Girl Scout camping trips. "I guess I did forget," he admitted, running a hand through his hair in frustration. "But it's the worst possible timing," James groaned.

"Honey, you just can't get out of it now. It's too late to find a substitute. The girls in her group won't be able to go without you." Carol added, "And I can't cover you on this one! You know I promised Tommy I'd take him and a friend to that new IMAX Adventure, and then I told them they could have a sleepover here."

James looked at the ceiling, groaned out loud in frustration, and threw his hands out in surrender, "All right, all right. Fine." Just what he needed, his work life was coming down around his ears, and he was going to have to spend the next two days with six adolescent girls in a canoe.

He went upstairs to pack for the trip. He jerked his duffel bag out of his closet, threw it on the bed in annoyance and began packing. After he finished stuffing his clothes into the duffel bag, because who cared about wrinkles anyway, James sent out a few e-mails giving instructions to the team while he was out on Friday.

The next morning, James woke Susan up early, and they were out the door before seven o'clock. They drove to the middle school where a bus was waiting to pick up all of the girls and chaperones to shuttle them to the canoeing launch site on the Etowah River.

The trip up took almost three hours and was miserable for James. Susan had just reached that age where Dad was no longer cool to be around, so she spent most of the trip doing everything possible to avoid sitting with him or having a conversation with him.

The other chaperones were nice enough, but the leader, Miss Ellen, was a bit gung-ho for James' taste. Besides, James was pretty preoccupied with the situation at the plant. He found his thoughts wandering in and out of the conversations he was having. He kept replaying in his mind the conversation with Jennings, and his options.

Upon arrival at the launch area, James gratefully exited the small rickety bus and stood at the door helping the girls jump down from the bottom step. After the last girl was off the bus, he resigned himself to a miserable day. Inevitably, someone always managed to "accidentally" fall in and get wet. That always made for "girl drama" as his son frequently called it.

James looked around, assessing the area, and organized his daughter's group. He herded them over to the outfitter's shed to get their gear. James was annoyed to discover that the gear was damp, musty smelling, and a bit moldy. The canoes and paddles looked a little worse for wear as well he noticed. Miss Ellen had apparently decided to go budget.

"Miss Ellen would certainly be Jennings' favorite Scout leader," James muttered under his breath sarcastically.

The girls were outfitted with their gear, complaining about their smelly, dank life vests, while frequently dissolving into fits of giggles. The high pitched giggles grated on James' already frazzled nerves, but he smiled indulgently when Susan turned to make sure he was still there. They finally hoisted the canoe onto their shoulders and marched off to the launch point.

When James had the canoe situated at the water line, he held it steady while each of the girls boarded, scrambled to their seats, and grabbed up their paddles in excitement. When they were all loaded and seated, James pushed the canoe into the water before jumping into the back of the canoe. With his added weight, the craft instantly listed to one side as they all let out a collective groan. It seemed to sit too low in the water, and unless James was missing something, there was a slow leak. He got back out, and pulled the loaded canoe on to the shore, telling the girls he'd be right back.

He approached the outfitter, hoping for a replacement canoe, but she assured him that all the canoes were spoken for. James did a quick assessment of the other five canoes in their party, which were just launching, and decided that theirs was far from the worst. They would just have to make do.

James pushed off and boarded the canoe again. They drifted close to the shoreline, with all the other filled canoes, as the group leader spent about ten minutes giving some quick lessons and going over the rules. After a few last instructions and many impatient snorts from the girls, they were off. The girls sat side-by-side on the three benches to paddle, and James sat in the back to paddle, as well as steer. The plan was to go downstream several miles negotiating a couple of small rapids and have lunch in a pre-designated clearing. After lunch, they would try their hand at a couple of larger rapids and finish the day on a long flat part of the river that came to the meadow where the cabins would be waiting for their overnight stay.

Immediately, James saw that the canoe was going to be an issue. When the girls paddled, the boat rocked, and with the list and the low draft, water was seeping in over the sides. The more water in the boat, the lower it would ride and the worse things were going to get. Of course, the little leak in the back was not helping things either. It was obvious that someone was going to have to be assigned to get the water out of the boat as they made their way downriver.

James asked Brooke, one of the smaller girls, to start bailing. Unfortunately, they only had a small cup, so Brooke bailed as fast as she could but could barely keep up with the water coming in. James looked up to see that several of the canoes had already designated a full-time bailer.

The system worked well enough until they hit the first rapid. The extra force of the water meant that the canoe was even less stable and more water came in. The bailer worked at an ever more frantic pace but could not keep up, and as the water rose in the bottom, the edges of the canoe sank lower and lower until it was almost flush with the waterline. Additionally, the bailer was bailing so fast with her little cup that she was also destabilizing the boat, and it was not clear to James whether the water going out from bailing was more than what was coming in from her rocking of the boat.

When they exited the rapids, they could no longer see Miss Ellen's lead boat, and there was ankle deep water in the boat, which of course had the girls complaining about their cold feet. It was clear that one bailer was not going to be enough. Great, thought James, another day and a half of this.

James motioned to Susan, "Susie, I'm going to need you to bail too. Get your cup out."

"But, Daaaad," Susan wailed, "I want to paddle. You're in charge so can't you make someone else do it?"

James blanched when Susie actually batted her eyelashes and looked at him beseechingly. He wondered where his little girl had learned the fine art of manipulating the opposite sex.

He shook his head no and resolved to stand firm. "Susie, we're going to sink if you don't help bail. I am not in charge right now, the water is in charge. And the water is saying we need to get the boat cleared out before the next rapid," James replied.

Susie scowled at him and reluctantly reached for her cup as she got down on the floor of the boat with Brooke and started bailing. After ten minutes, they could hear the next rapid in the distance, which was the final obstacle before lunch.

"You're doing great, girls!" James cheered encouragingly. "You've almost hit the goal of having the boat cleared before the next rapid!"

"Dad," Susie replied with typical adolescent disdain, "the goal isn't to bail out the boat. The goal is to have fun paddling through the rapids." Susan pierced him with an icy stare, apparently waiting for his response.

James was taken aback. He flashed back to a conversation with Chance. Of course, she was right. The goal was not to bail. Bailing was just a means. The goal was to get to their destination with the rest of their troop, have fun, and learn something while doing it.

"You're right, honey. Forget the bailing, girls. Everyone grab a paddle for the next rapid and get ready to paddle."

Brooke and Susie both excitedly jumped up to grab their paddles, causing the canoe to rock crazily as every girl in the boat squealed and grabbed the sides of the boat for stability, one or two almost losing their paddles in the process. James, wincing at the shrill noise, shot an arm out to steady Susie, barely saving her from flipping head first out of the canoe, while Brooke sheepishly settled herself on the seat and began paddling. When Susie finally sat down with her paddle and started paddling, James breathed a sigh of relief.

"Whew," James said out loud, "that was a close call." His only response was a giggle from Susie. The girls paddled furiously as he concentrated on steering through the quickly approaching rapids.

They made their way through the rapids, sloshing from side to side. With no bailer, the water level in the canoe quickly rose. They exited the rapid barely afloat with almost a foot of water in the bottom of the canoe. But James was gratified to see the huge grins on every face as they pulled up to the lunch site alongside the other canoes.

James held the canoe steady and helped each girl to jump out. He quickly turned the canoe over to drain the water and then noticed many of the other girls were already eating. They must have been there for some time.

Miss Ellen greeted them with a look and a shake of the head. "James, I see you are in the back of the pack," she said disapprovingly.

The smiles instantly dropped from the girls' faces, and James heard numerous complaints about being last, not having time to spend with their friends, not having time to eat their lunch. It went on and on.

Great, thought James to himself, I'm in the back of the pack even in Girl Scouts. He thought that the one saving grace of this trip would be to take his mind off of work. James dragged the canoe further out of the water and headed for the food.

Over lunch, James thought of little else but work. What was he going to do with the failing planned initiative? How was he going to get the cost initiative done? Should he even do it? What was the future of the shadow network and their efforts? Should he beef it up or shut it down?

Next his thoughts drifted to the canoe and how he might make the girls' experience better. He knew they had to find a way to get the water out faster. He thought about a lot of alternatives. If only they had a foot pump or some bigger containers to bail with. Maybe he needed three girls to bail on the rough parts. Yeah, that would make him really popular.

The rest of the day was more of the same, leaky boat, bottom full of water, bailer working frantically. Sometimes they went with one bailer and other times with two. As he watched the girls bailing on the last leg, he could not help but be reminded of his maintenance team. They were just like the bailers, rushing to where the water was in an attempt to take care of the problem and keep the plant afloat. But, just like the bailers, the maintenance employees frenetic rushing around, at times, made things worse, not better.

As they drifted along the last, flat stretch on the way to the campsite, James made a point to encourage the girls.

"You guys did a great job today. I appreciate you putting up with the problems with the canoe. I promise tomorrow will be better. Tonight I'm going to work on finding us a bigger bucket to bail with, even if I have to hike up to get it."

"Dad," Susan asked, "why don't we just figure out a way to keep the water from coming in the boat in the first place? That would be a lot more fun."

James thought for a moment, and it became blindingly obvious. His solution with the bigger bucket was really no different from Robert, MRS, and their planned maintenance. Their focus was entirely on taking defects out faster and more efficiently. Certainly that would be better than the reactive small cup they had been using. With a bucket, they would do a better job of staying afloat, but the water would still be coming in and still be in charge. Susan's idea sounded just like the plant manager's from St. Louis, "We'll breakdown everything we're doing…and work to eliminate every source of failure." Frankly, it was a lot like the operator PM program and the action teams that were going on at the plant. The answer seemed clear. Keep the water from coming in the boat in the first place.

For the rest of the flat water, they worked on their stroke technique to get the rolling and surges out of their gait. James also figured out that if he placed the two bumper buoys in the boat below the water line and strapped them to the boat in just the right places, he could get the front end to rise up about an inch higher from the waterline, which took out the list. With these adjustments, all six girls paddled rapidly and happily to the overnight campsite.

The next day was brilliant. With all six girls paddling, and the canoe riding high, they were able to grab the lead from Miss Ellen who was still struggling with a bailer for many sections. The girls were having a blast, and James had to admit he was enjoying himself as well.

As they were loading the canoes back onto the outfitter's trailer at the end of the day, James realized he had barely thought about work all day. He felt much clearer about the path forward than he had in weeks. He leaned over and kissed Susan on the top of the head, "Keep the water from coming in the boat in the first place, and don't let the water be in charge. Brilliant!" he whispered.

She looked up at him quizzically, "Please, Dad! Get it together."

She ran off to talk to her friends, as James chuckled to himself. And they'd even made it through the trip with no spills in the drink!

PUTTING THE PIECES TOGETHER

On Monday, James was at the plant earlier than usual. He took some time to draw out his plan on paper and faxed a copy of it to Chance. He had sent a message to the members of his shadow network to meet in the conference room first thing. He had also invited Vance and Buzz.

While everyone filed into the room, Chance connected by teleconference. When everyone was seated, James began, "After the meeting at headquarters, I had the weekend to reflect on where we are and what we have in front of us. We have the planned maintenance initiative which is frankly struggling."

When Vance visibly winced at this remark, James averted his gaze and resolved to continue. He would not normally have been so direct with front-line operators and mechanics in the room, but James needed to make his point. "The cost initiative that we've laid out in response to Jennings' request will most certainly reduce cost, but it isn't going to get any of us a plant that we're proud of, and the network team that's been working on operator PMs and the like is too small to make any real difference.

"However, the one thing they all have in common is defects. The planned maintenance initiative is all about how to get defects out more effectively and efficiently, with the cost initiative, the costs that we lag on versus our peers are driven by defects, and the network team has focused on eliminating sources of defects.

"Well, my eyes were opened over the weekend, and I see clearly now that defects are our enemy. We need a full court press on wiping those suckers out. We're the leaders and the managers in this plant, but we are not in control, the defects are. Steve, when you called that crew out on a Sunday a few months back, is that really what you wanted to do?"

"No," responded Steve hesitantly, not knowing exactly where the question was leading.

"Exactly! But since the defects are in control, you called them out anyway. We're not going to reach our goals until we take control of the defects. Let me share my idea for a plan of attack." James walked over to the flip chart and pointed to the drawing on it.

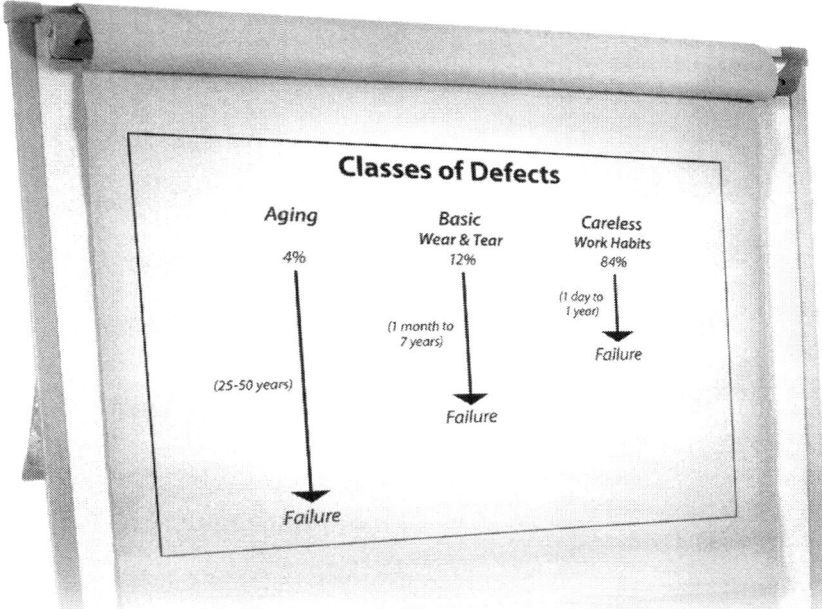

These three types of defects, which we've discussed before, are all direct results of operating equipment for its purpose or goal, which is to meet the needs of our customers. As we've also discussed, defects left untreated get worse over time and lead to failures. Failures come in all forms, from catastrophic line stoppages to small leaks that waste product or energy." James paused to flip to the second page on the flip chart.

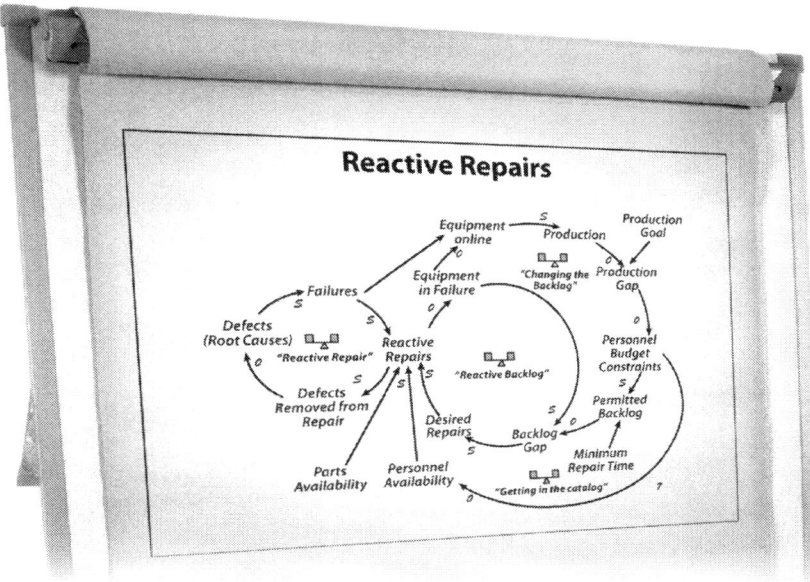

"We work very hard in maintenance to eliminate these defects, after a failure, in the case of a reactive scenario, or before a failure, in a planned scenario. However, despite best intentions, we add defects back through poor workmanship and parts. As we saw in the forensic analysis, these come in at a pretty great rate. All that maintenance work takes time and money, and the failures and down time cost us production and waste. I believe we've been too focused these last six months on improving the repair loop, and we haven't spent nearly enough time in eliminating the sources of defects." James stopped to let the message sink in then flipped to the next page on the flip chart.

At the top of the page, he had written in big letters, "Integrate Production, Cost, and Maintenance Improvements by Eliminating the Sources of Defects." There were several bullets listed.

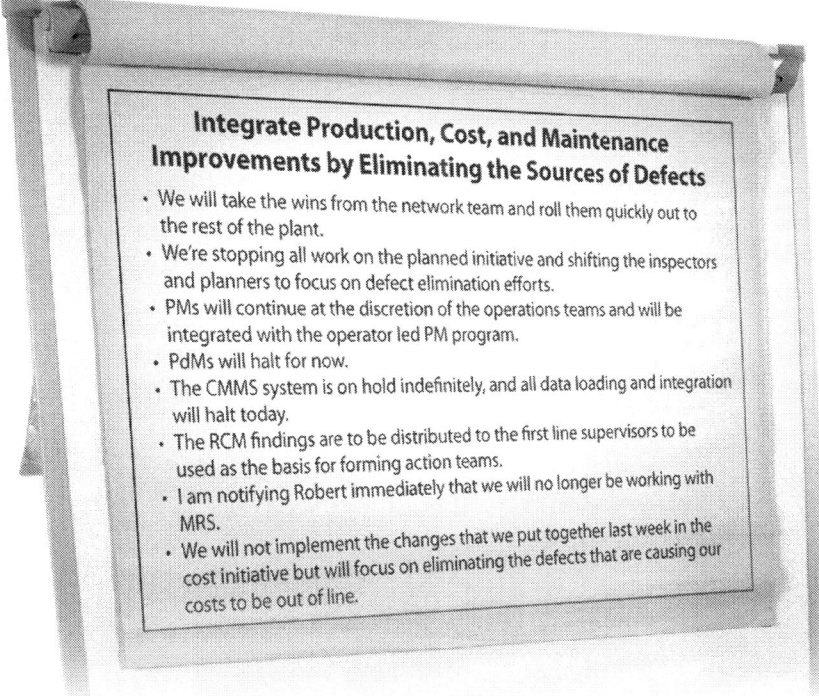

"Guys, I know this is a big change, and we all put a lot of work into different aspects of these plans, but we have to face the facts. If we don't eliminate the sources of the work and costs, we are only going to make limited and temporary improvements."

When James finished, the room was silent.

Buzz was the first to comment, "We have to try something different, and I have to admit this makes sense. I'm on board. Do you think Jennings will let you do this?"

"Let me worry about Jennings. I just need to know if you guys think this is the right focus," James said.

Heads around the room nodded in unison. They were all smiling. Everyone wanted to paddle, and no one wanted to bail. Except Vance, of course, he sat silently, stone faced.

Ignoring Vance, James continued, "Great! Lorraine is setting up a series of development and kick-off meetings and will give you each the schedule."

They all got up to leave, but when James headed out Vance followed him. He stood in the middle of James' office with his arms crossed.

"James, how could you undercut me like that? How do you expect me to be effective when you kill my program in a public setting?"

"I'm sorry for that, Vance, but we need to get moving now, and I need to make sure everyone is on board. What do you think of the plan?"

"Well, frankly, I think it's daffy. You haven't given the planned initiative time to succeed, and you're tossing it out right as we're getting it refined. If you would just give some backbone to the program and make Buzz's team comply, we could get over the hump."

"No, that's where you're wrong, Vance. I thought the same thing for a long time but even perfectly executed, I don't think it's the right direction. We don't need to bail the boat faster. We need to shut down the leaks. I need you to be 100% on board, or I need you to look for an appropriate transfer," James added firmly.

Vance clenched his jaw and glared at James, "I'll call HR this afternoon and inquire about a transfer." Vance spun on his heel and immediately left the office as James sighed in frustration. Why did this always have to be so hard?

James got up to close his door. He clenched his fists in frustration as he plopped back into his chair and stared at the shield logo on his bulletin board. After a few moments of trying to calm down, James realized that he honestly felt more relief than disappointment at Vance's decision. He needed to insure the safety of his employees, and Vance was never going to understand that concept. He wished he'd had the gumption to control Vance's actions a little better. He'd let him sabotage his plans for far too long.

As the week progressed, James resolved to see who among his staff would be the best candidate for the new maintenance manager position.

The more he thought about it, the more excited he became when Steve Sarkey came to his attention. The position was a perfect opportunity for Steve, his maintenance supervisor, and his most trusted ally in the shadow network. Although he didn't have management experience, he was completely on board with the inspections and defect elimination process James had been touting.

Although they had improved the efficiency of the maintenance staff in the past few months, the years of neglect were starting to catch up to them. He realized that they needed to double their efforts for a few more months before things would really become better.

They also needed to create a culture of defect elimination. He knew that a new maintenance manager was the least of his needs. The maintenance manager could not do it alone. He would need to be confident enough to allow front line workers to make their own decisions but still keep folks on track. It was a political game, really, and Steve would be perfect.

That had been the problem with Vance. He had been so power hungry that he micromanaged everything. James grimaced as he realized he walked that fine line himself. He knew that it wasn't about power in his case. It was simply that his feelings about safety often made him more controlling than he wanted to be. James was constantly checking himself to allow others to work independently. He knew Steve would be on board all the way with him. He would just have to convince everyone that Steve was perfect for the job. He sighed as he headed out to the floor to check on things. He had a lot of work to do.

The meeting the following week was not any easier. Robert, the MRS consultant, was at first in disbelief. He tried to talk James out of what he called "a rash action", then tried to negotiate a fee reduction, and finally threatened to go to Jennings directly. James informed him that he had told Jennings his plan last night and that while he was not thrilled, he was committed to giving James some rope. Even if it was just to hang himself, James thought.

By noon, James had cleared the decks and was able to take a call from Chance.

"Well, James, that was quite a leap you took today. You must know how Cortez felt when he burned his ships after arriving in the New World. The message to his men was clear. There was only one direction to go, and that's forward. From my perspective, you nailed it. I didn't want to encourage you to drop formal corporate initiatives, but I have to admit, I was having trouble figuring out how you were going to pull them all off. Integrating them into one idea was a brilliant stroke."

They talked at length about the path forward and what the right first steps would be.

Chance had one more piece of news, "I have been working with the folks from MIT, and I think we have a great cut at our version of the Beer Distribution Game for manufacturing reliability. It really drives the key points home. I think you're going to love it. I would like to come down next week and give it a try as a kick-off to launching the action teams that you're talking about."

"Excellent," replied James. "I'll clear my schedule to be available as well."

Vance's transfer was complete within three weeks of his initial request, having landed a job as the maintenance manager at the Houston plant. James was thrilled that Vance's timely exit was in perfect timing for Steve's approved promotion to the maintenance manager position. It would be great to have an ally on defect elimination.

One Monday morning in early September, Chance came down with the professor, Mark Sterman, and his research assistant, to launch the first set of teams with their board game simulation that they were calling The Defect Elimination Game[2]. They'd invited five action teams from the plant to participate, which accounted for thirty of the participants. Six people from the leadership team made up the remainder of the participants.

The game itself was still a bit crude and a work-in-progress, but it was a smash hit none the less. The MIT team had decided to use different colored poker chips to represent the various aspects of the plant. There was an area of the 4' by 6' game board focused on operating the plant, a section dedicated to maintenance, and a section dedicated to the finances and business aspects of the plant. Each game board fit on a large table and a team of six (two in each area) sat around each board and performed as the operating team. The equipment, which was in the center of the operations area, was represented by black poker chips, and the defects that came from all of the various sources identified earlier in the modeling effort were red and stamped with different colored bugs that showed what their root cause was, such as workmanship, design, wear and tear, mis operations, etc.

The plant started off very reactively with bugs everywhere. The objective of the game was to improve the plant's production performance but also to manage costs. Participants had to make a lot of the same decisions that the leaders of the real plant faced:

- How to allocate operations' time between operating the plant, dealing with broken equipment, helping with planned maintenance,

[2]The Defect Elimination Game, the game first described as the game created by MIT is based on The Manufacturing Game® To get more information about The Manufacturing Game®, go to www.ManufacturingGame.com

or working on improvements.
- How to allocate maintenance time between fixing broken equipment, moving into planned activities or investing in improvements.
- If the team would invest in eliminating defects, which ones would they focus on and why?
- There were trade-offs to be made between making the weekly production and adhering to planned maintenance schedules.
- There was a storeroom of parts to manage. Did the team focus on availability of parts or on financial metrics?

These decisions drove differences in the results of the plant: how much money was made, the achievement of production goals, frequency of safety and environmental incidents, and the cost structure. Participants operated these virtual plants for thirty-five weeks of simulated time over a one-day session. They got to call all of the shots and see the implications of their decisions.

James was thoroughly enjoying himself as he played. He was in the operations role and was desperate to try the defect source elimination investments that were built into the game. He was struggling, however, because his resources were absorbed in fighting virtual fires and operating the plant. Reese, the operations supervisor in the real plant, was playing on another team in the maintenance role. He was getting a kick out of watching James struggle with all of the same trade-offs that he faced on a daily basis.

All six teams struggled, but by the end of the thirty-five simulated weeks, each had made a dramatic transformation in their plants. As they debriefed, they talked about the results and how they achieved them.

An operator from one of the action teams stated, "We more than doubled our profits during the game. Our production was 20% higher, and our costs were actually lower than when we started."

Later, during the debrief session, Reese made a comment, "I was struck by how hard it was to make decisions in maintenance, and how frustrating it was when operations did not do what we needed them to do to stick to the plan. The shoe was really on the other foot, and I was able to see all of the problems that I personally create in operations when I'm short sighted."

A mechanic that was on one of the action teams added, "It was really hard to move into planned maintenance. We invested early but didn't see any benefits. In fact, costs actually went up for a while, and it was awfully tempting to cut it back when we were feeling financial pressure. But we stuck with it, and it sure seemed to pay-off in the end. By the end of the game, our plant was not doing any reactive work. It makes me wonder if the shift away from planned maintenance is really the right move for the real plant. Have we just not been patient long enough?"

James was itching to answer but didn't want to come off as sounding defensive. Fortunately, the stores clerk who had been his partner in operations chimed in, "Well, we took a different approach. We agreed not to focus on planned maintenance and put most of our effort into defect elimination. It really paid off. What shocked us the most was that at the end of the game, when we decided to add planned maintenance, it was a snap to implement and had really quick returns. I don't think it is a matter of "if" it is a good idea. Of course a planned plant is better than a reactive one. It's just a matter of sequence."

"Oh yeah," the mechanic replied who had made the original point about planning, "defect elimination was the key. There is no doubt about that. We saw the whole plant turn as we started shutting down the flow of defects."

At that remark, James decided to chime in. "But it was much more difficult than I imagined. It was hard to muster the resources to get the improvements made. It seemed like there was always something more urgent that got in the way. But once you got to a certain point it really just took off."

Mark Sterman picked up on James' point, "That's the nature of this system. There are a series of reinforcing relationships centered mostly on how defects are added. When you cut down the number of failures, you really kick in a series of virtuous cycles that makes improvement accelerate. Did anyone feel like they gained any insight into which defect source to focus on first?"

"Our team did something interesting," volunteered one of the operators who was scheduled to be on an action team. "We piled up the defects as we took them out, and since they were all color coded by source, it was like a root cause analysis. We found that the defects from operations were the most important."

"That's consistent with the data and model that we've been working on," agreed Mark.

The conversation went on for some time. It was clear that the lessons had sunk in and made an impact with people. Even the team that had been intimately involved in the modeling learned a great deal. The noise level in the room was high as folks were laughing and arguing game techniques when one of the operators raised his hands to quiet everyone.

"This game was fine and all, but for the guys working in the field, it didn't tell us anything that we didn't already know. We've been trying to get some of these dumb defects out of here for years, but management will never give us the time or the money to take care of it. There's always some cost cutting effort, or other initiative, that gets in the way. We never have time to fix it right, but we always seem to have time to fix it again and again."

There were a lot of heads nodding in agreement throughout the room. James again felt naturally defensive but did not want to squash the enthusiasm in the room. One of the mechanics picked up on the point.

"I agree, man, but it's not even just a matter of fixing it right. If we want to do what we did in the game, we have to fix it right and eliminate the defects that caused it in the first place - don't just fix it…improve it."

"Hey, I like that," James jumped in. "That's exactly the mentality we have to create in everyone in the plant. Let me take that back to the leadership team. I hear what all of you are saying, and I want to provide more authority for you to fix things right and eliminate defects. The good news is that our next agenda item for the workshop is to break into teams and tackle a specific defect in your area. If you've been a frustrated defect eliminator, you now have an opportunity to take action and make a difference. For my team, we'll work on how to make 'Don't Just Fix It… Improve It' part of our operating practice." With that, James turned the workshop back over to the facilitators.

When the action teams broke out and started working on their tasks, Reese was amazed at how little direction they needed. They knew what management was after, they understood what defects were, they had a laundry list of defects to address, and once they chose one, they had very concrete views on how to eliminate them. Some needed a bit of help putting together specific actions and aggressive timelines to get the defect eliminated, but it was a far cry from the efforts he had had to expend on previous teams. If they could launch teams this easily and with this much clarity, it would be easily sustainable.

After the workshop, the team from the shadow network got together with the facilitators from MIT and suggested a series of tweaks for the game, as well as the workshop, but everyone agreed that it would be an important tool for rolling out the coming changes and the action teams.

Five months into the new plan, James was starting to see momentum build. With the help of The Defect Elimination Game workshops, they had launched over sixty defect elimination action teams in the plant. Just like the action teams in the Extrusion line, these teams were successfully eliminating small defects all over the plant.

The Defect Elimination Game had been a great addition by Chance. It showed participants the journey from the Reactive Domain to the Precision Domain, and more importantly, it gave the participants a chance to experiment with the levers to see how to get there. The bottom line message was clear to everyone who attended a workshop. Eliminate the source of defects and your life at the plant, along with every measure of performance, will improve.

They were also using the workshops as a way to re-enforce the concept of the "Don't Just Fix it, Improve It" message. They handed out a poker chip that had a bug representing a defect with a line through it "Ghost Buster's style" to each participant at the end of the Defect Elimination Game session. On the back was the phrase, "Don't Just Fix It, Improve It". They encouraged the participants to pull out the token any time they were being pressured to patch something up, or simply fix it, without eliminating the underlying cause, and challenge management to walk the talk.

There were already dozens of stories circulating about reluctant managers who gave in and allowed the team a little more time or a little more money to drive out the defect. It was not without problems. Supervisors and managers felt that giving the front line workers so much authority reduced their power. Many were frustrated that their decision making was being undermined by this implicit promise to the front-line that they could challenge any directives that did not eliminate the root cause.

James struggled with this at first. His inclination was to get involved and find a happy medium, but in the end, as he listened to the situations, he found that in most cases the front-line was toeing the line on the philosophy and culture more than the supervisors. If he stopped or overruled the challenges, he would squelch out the culture he was trying to create. He came up with a pat answer for supervisors, "It is still your area and you ultimately make the calls. However, if your team is challenging you to eliminate a defect, and you are pushing for a short term benefit over defect elimination, then you really need to look at your own priorities and not push the issue to your area manager or me."

Cindy had taken ownership of forming the teams and had based many of her teams on findings from the RCM analysis. The shadow network, now with over fifty participants, had debated this action team selection process. Cindy had lobbied for the defects and teams to be picked ahead of time to maximize the impact of the efforts, but many in the network, including Chance, felt that the teams should pick their own defects to ensure that they had the passion to complete the project. It would mean more to them if they chose a defect that affected them personally.

Chance told James that it was important to be very careful when the goal was to engage the entire organization. He went on to explain that when a manager tried to control the actions too much from the top, it killed the passion of the effort. James agreed with Chance's advice. He might have to give up some efficiency as a result, but he felt that the positive impact of having everyone engaged was more than worth it.

The shadow network came up with a workable compromise that James was comfortable with. The teams would be chosen around a particular area, problem, or piece of equipment, and be invited to the workshop as a group so that they would have the required skills to eliminate the defects. Cindy would provide them with suggested topics, including topics from the RCMs. However, the team was free to select any defect it wished, including defects completely off of the topic given.

The payoff for this approach was apparent just a few weeks later. An action team had been formed in the mixing line, and Cindy made the suggestion that they work on the main drive of one of the mixers. The team mulled over the issues for a bit, but they were not very excited about any of the potential defects. In fact, there were a couple of long-time employees on the team who were skeptical of the whole process and were not really participating in the discussions.

When one of them made an off-handed comment about management not being very serious about defect elimination, one of the other team members challenged him.

"Why would you say that? They've certainly dedicated a lot of time and resources to eliminating defects."

The older, crotchety operator replied, "If they were serious, they'd do something about the butane pressure vessel. Someone is going to get killed one of these days if we don't get that under control."

The team then had a heated debate about the problem with the vessel. Apparently, all of the operators knew it had been a long-standing problem, but all of their requests for capital had been denied going back almost ten years. The team decided right then and there to dump their suggested topic and take on the pressure vessel, if for no other reason than to test whether management was sincere.

Within a week, they found that the problem was temperature build up. They recruited an engineer to the team to help determine the underlying cause of the defect. They found that the cooler was undersized and needed to be replaced. They submitted a capital request for $25,000 and were denied on the grounds that they didn't show adequate return.

But the team refused to give up. They were now convinced that it was an important defect. The three lead mechanics on the team each had a three thousand dollar authority for repairs. They convinced the vendor to sell them the cooler in components over three weeks, with each component under the three thousand dollar limit. This was a very clear violation of the spirit of the signature authority rules, but the mechanics decided to take the personal risk to eliminate the defect. Once the new cooler was installed, there was an almost immediate drop in temperature and pressure.

The real impact was seen about a week later. Another action team had been working on eliminating waste to the incinerator and had been tracking root causes of how things got to the incinerator. The week that the new cooler was installed, the action team saw a significant drop in the flow to the incinerator. When they investigated the root cause, they found that the operators on the mixing line, aware that the butane vessel was an issue, had instituted an informal and undocumented practice of opening a relief valve from the vessel to the incinerator three times a shift to keep the pressure within limits. No one had thought to document or include these losses in the previous capital requests, but the waste team had documented them and calculated that the annual cost of the lost feedstock was worth over one million dollars.

When James heard the story of the team and their impact, he was thrilled. He immediately scheduled a plant-wide celebration. He made a big production out of the tenacity of this team and their passion for eliminating this defect. He thanked the crotchety old operator for challenging the earnestness of the management team and picking a defect that was meaningful to him. He thanked the mechanics for bending the rules to get the defect eliminated. He emphasized that the rules were there for a reason, and under no circumstances should anyone violate a rule that could jeopardize safety, but if a rule was getting in the way of eliminating a defect they should challenge it. At the end, James invited the entire team up to the front of the shop and Steve rolled out a human-sized replica of the bug that he and Reese had created for the hard hats back at the Extrusion line. It was built around a punching bag. James pulled out a Louisville slugger and gave each team member a turn slugging the giant bug. The last operator, a big burly guy from southern Georgia, whacked it so hard that three legs flew off. The whole place went nuts and the meeting was adjourned.

Steve and Buzz collaborated to get the operator PM program up throughout the plant and were having success similar to the first two lines they'd attempted. They always started with a massive clean-up of the area where they would eliminate a lot of small defects that had built up. Reese would often lead these sessions with the same mantra he had used on the Extrusion line, "You can't eliminate a defect you can't see."

The operators would make small changes, using the Extrusion line as an example, to make it easier to spot defects, and create a shift-based PM routine to check all of the inspection points. Invariably, they would also come up with a list of defects too big to tackle as part of the PM effort. Steve would feed these to Cindy as fodder for new action teams.

James heard comments from participants like, "The game quickly shows how much the entire plant suffers when a reactive approach is taken versus a proactive approach," and "The game shows how cross functional improvement teams can quickly solve issues and add value to all areas of the plant."

His store room supervisor even stated, "The game shows how a limited inventory, or even the possibility of having zero inventory, could be achieved through a planned and proactive maintenance route."

Some participants had been extremely skeptical and couldn't understand how a game would help them in their everyday jobs. When they came out of the workshops, they had a whole new outlook. The game gave participants a bird's eye view of how the decisions they made affected others, and there was more consideration being given to other departments when decisions were made.

It was too early to call it a success, but James had to admit he liked what he was hearing and seeing. He was beginning to see the light at the end of the tunnel.

Chapter 9

Engaging the Organization

The defect elimination approach had been in full swing for almost seven months when James received the latest scorecard results. He was relieved that the results were really starting to turn around. Yes, he'd thought the same thing when the last scorecard came out, but he really believed they would surpass the performance level that they had reached at the peak of the MRS program. And best of all, Jennings was finally off of James' back, which was a huge relief. With the state of the economy, James knew people's jobs were in jeopardy. They needed to be performing at an optimal performance level and James felt a responsibility to his employees to make sure they all had jobs.

Everyone in the plant, from the plant manager right down to the assistants, had been through The Defect Elimination Game and participated on an action team. In fact, James had started mixing in key suppliers, some of the outside repair shops they used, the sales and marketing team and even two key customers. Cindy had started tracking the teams and their results. Over one hundred twenty teams had been formed, mostly out of the workshops, but a number had just popped up spontaneously. That was the topic of today's shadow network conversation, "How to keep up the momentum of the action teams now that the workshops were complete?"

In a great mood after reviewing the scorecard numbers, James headed to the conference room for the scheduled shadow network meeting. When Cindy took the floor, James was pleased to hear that in preparation for the meeting, Cindy had taken the time to look at each of the twenty-five or so "organic" teams that had come together on their own without being formed in a workshop. She'd even interviewed the participants so she could report back to the shadow group.

"The story was almost always the same," Cindy said with a big grin on her face. "Someone on the team, and sometimes multiple members, had gotten fired up. These people are real 'go-getters.' They went out and recruited others to tackle new defects." Cindy ended her presentation by noting, "It seems that becoming a 'go-getter' is a bit contagious. People at all levels, with all different levels of experience, and frankly, all different sorts of attitudes have become 'go-getters'. The thing they all have in common is that someone on their original team was a 'go-getter', and they were inspired by that person. The second thing they have in common is that they got excited about making a difference."

Chance chimed in, "That feels right based on my own experiences. We had the exact same thing happen in St. Louis. The majority of our personnel are what you're calling 'go-getters'. In my experience, the average plant has just 10-20% of people who are out there making improvements on their own initiative. Usually 60-70% will go along with management and 10-20% of them are openly hostile. But the real magic happens when you get 60%, or more, on the side of making proactive improvements. You're never going to get everyone, but there's is a real tipping point when you get to more than 50%. And you've hit the nail on the head, Cindy, it's absolutely contagious."

"That gives me two thoughts," James spoke up. "First, this notion of creating 'go-getters' reminds me of a survey question that MRS asked. It really bothered me at the time. Over a year ago, they asked people if they were actively working to improve the plant. I don't remember the exact words but that's the gist of it. I remember being disappointed to see that only 10% answered that question positively. I would love to see what that number is now. I think we should track that measure quarterly as part of the HR process. Let's start with this quarter. Second, how do we create an environment where this contagion spreads quickly?"

"If I may?" interrupted one of the HR associates in the room. "As some of you know, my last job was with the Centers for Disease Control here in Atlanta. We always had it drilled into us that contagions are driven by three factors. The first is the virulence of the germ. You know, how easy it is to catch and transmit. The second is the duration of the contagious period, and the third is the contact rate between the infected and the uninfected. It is usually the third element that the CDC focuses on when they are trying to limit an infection. So, based on my experience with that, I've been tracking that number for a while now, and the current ownership figure is 96%. So that's a huge improvement over the 10% you mentioned that MRS tracked more than a year ago." She opened her folder and pulled out a piece of paper with a graph tracking the ownership percentages.

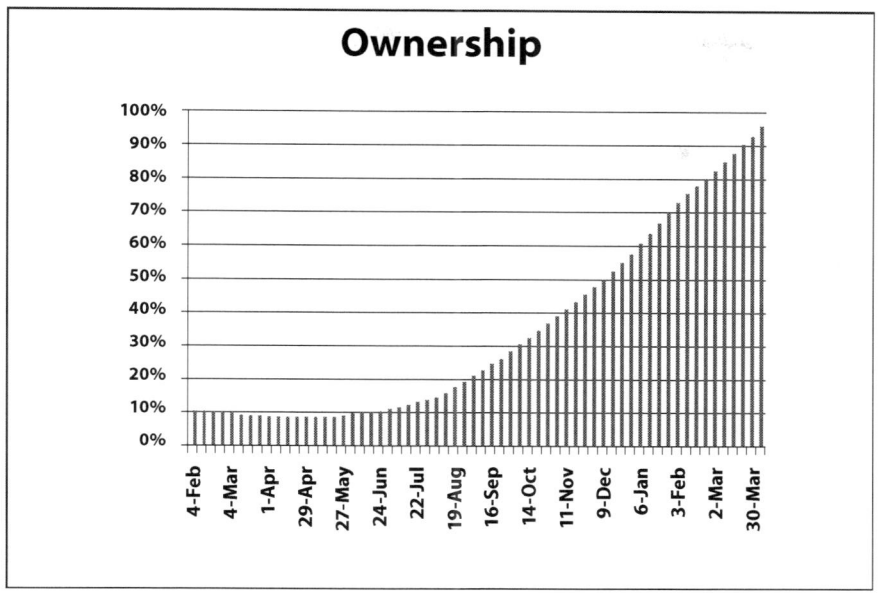

Chance and James both leaned in to look at the graph. They broke out into huge smiles as James pointed to a spot on the page. James picked up the graph and turned it around for all to see.

"Look at this folks! You probably can't see these dates down here," pointing to the graph, "but let me point out this date right here, July 22nd. That's when we stopped the MRS program, and we began the defect elimination program full scale."

James noted the shocked expressions on many faces around the table. Even James himself was a bit shocked. He put the paper down and wrote the figures from the graph onto his copy of the current scorecard.

"We certainly need to track this figure in our future scorecards. We want to make sure this number doesn't drop."

\multicolumn{4}{c}{**Atlanta Scorecard 5: April 7th**}
Key Performance Indicator	**Description**	**Atlanta Plant Current Year Forecast**	**Best in Class**
Maintenance as a % of Replacement Value	Maintenance cost, excluding capital compared to the estimated capital cost to replace the plant equipment	3.8%	2%
Overtime %	Percent of overtime for hourly workers	23%	<5%
Waste cost as a percent of raw materials cost	The cost of all scrap and defective output compared to total input	1.5%	0.2%
Raw material cost per ton of output	Applied only to plants making similar outputs	$19.09	$20
Labor cost per ton of output	Applied only to plants making similar outputs	$11.94	$7.30
Consumables, parts and outside repairs cost per ton		$5.17	$2.50
Energy costs per ton		$7.48	$7.25
% Planned Maintenance Work	% of work that is planned and scheduled at least 1 week in advance	64%	95%
Production % of Max	Maximum production the plant can operate at	81%	98%
Earnings	Last 12 months earnings in millions of dollars	$4.1 million (loss)	$40 million (profit)
Recordable injuries/ 200K man hours		1.07	<0.50
Ownership	*Employees actively look for ways to improve the plant*	*96%*	*>60%*

"That's great, and it's so helpful to have that quantified," Chance said. "So we know we have a concept in defect elimination that is easy to catch and transmit. People seem to stay enthused for at least a couple of months. The key is getting those 'go-getters' together with those who are less enthusiastic in an environment where their ownership of defect elimination can rub off on others."

"You know, we've done a good job of launching action teams from the workshops, but we don't have any formal process for doing it outside of the workshops. Maybe that's what we need. Something like a monthly Action Forum where we review current action teams, celebrate successes, and sponsor new teams," Cindy suggested.

"I like that idea," said Chance. "If I can, let me make a suggestion on attendance. In any attempt at change, you need three types of leadership. You need operational leaders who drive the action, network leaders who drive the ideas to pursue, and executive leaders who provide the vision and the resources. To have an effective Action Forum you need some of each. I would suggest having our operations supervisors involved as the operational leaders. Then Cindy, along with some of the engineers and maintenance folks, as the network leaders would be in charge of sifting through the ideas, and, of course, James, Buzz and Steve would provide the executive sponsorship."

James smiled feeling that progress was being made. "That sounds like a plan. I think we should ask each of our operations supervisors to bring a list of the top ten defects from their teams to work on in each session. We can bat around which ones make the most sense, pick the teams based on the defect, and make sure that we mix some of the 'go-getters' with the rest of the population to make sure we spread this ownership, or whatever you want to call it. Of course, just like before, the topics will merely be suggestions. The teams will still ultimately pick their own defects. Any objections?" As James looked around the room, he was pleased to see that there were no objections.

"Well, that brings me to my next two topics," Cindy announced. "While we've had over ninety-five teams complete their project and eliminate their defects, we don't have any type of formal reward or recognition program. Second, we have at least twenty teams that have basically failed. They have either abandoned their project or are simply making no progress. What should we do about those?"

James nodded, taking a moment to think. "I think we should let the Action Forum deal with reward and recognition. It sounds like the perfect place to do that. Regarding the failures, I'm just not sure. Chance, do you have any suggestions?"

"Sure," Chance answered. "Ignore the failures completely with one exception, make sure and track the root causes of your failures. I know that sounds wrong in a culture where we want to reward success and punish failure, but keep in mind our goals. We want to promote better plant performance through defect elimination. No one defect really makes much of a difference. Whether one particular team succeeds or fails is not really meaningful. The key is to get everyone eliminating defects every day, to take on that mantle of ownership that Cindy described earlier. Teams can fail for all sorts of reasons. They picked something too hard, the team had the wrong skills, the chemistry was bad, some management policy blocked them, you never know. You want to track these root causes without recrimination to make sure you don't have something structural blocking the way of our teams. Tracking and reviewing these obstacles can also be a role for the Action Forum. There ought to be a time in each meeting's agenda where you review the sources of team failures and decide what, if anything, management needs to do to remove obstacles."

"Hmm, you've made some very valid points, Chance. It sounds good," replied James. "I'll set up the first forum for next month. We'll invite the participants you recommended, Chance, and have the following agenda." James stood up to write on the dry eraser board, as he verbally ticked them off.

1. Review completed actions and celebrate successes.
2. Review teams that seem stuck and also the root cause of each.
3. Determine what action we need to take as a management team to eliminate recurring obstacles.
4. Engage the network leaders and the operational leaders in the selection of topics and teams for the following month.

Everyone quickly wrote down each item as they nodded their heads in agreement. The meeting adjourned and James headed to his office with a bounce in his step, feeling good about the decisions they had made that day.

Almost a month after the meeting of the shadow network where the ownership metric was introduced, they were holding their first action team forum. As James gathered up his files for the meeting, he took a moment to ponder how well things had been going since the shadow network meeting the month before. He was most proud of the fact that they had surpassed the ownership tipping point of 60% three months ago, and they were now holding steady at 96%.

As James left his office to kick-off the first Action Forum, he knew they needed to maintain the good attitudes while continuing to drive improvements in the other performance numbers. But the fact that they'd reached the goal of the leading indicator of success was a great sign. It was also looking like they just might make a profit this month.

At the meeting, James took a few minutes to recap the current action team results and made a point of calling out each of the operations supervisors as he talked about the action team in their area. Saving the best for last, he added, "We had twelve action teams complete their projects last month, so obviously we can't review all of them as we had planned. However, we have chosen five to review today, and we've also formed a smaller weekly forum to review and recognize the results of the others. And you know, the fact that we have more results than time to review, is a really great problem to have."

James introduced the members from the first team. It was a compressor team from the plating line.

Chuck, one of their seasoned operators, proudly stepped to the front to describe his team's efforts. "We picked a defect that was a vibration in the compressor. It had been bothering us since the accident with Todd because that team had ignored an ongoing vibration. Our team came in over a weekend when other equipment was being taken down. In fact, two of the guys on the team came in on their day off. We stripped the compressor down and found an odd geometric pitting on the main bearing. We called in all of the experts, but no one could explain the pitting on a bearing that was so new. We changed it out and hoped for the best.

"On start-up Monday morning, I noticed a spike in vibration that quickly settled down, but it was in the high end of the acceptable range. I logged the issue, and the team discussed it at shift change. We decided that it needed to come down again. It was not an easy sell, but Brian Evans, the operations supervisor, finally relented when I reminded him of the 'Don't Just Fix It, Improve It' slogan. When we took out the bearing, we found the same odd pitting. Again, no one could explain the cause. We were all pretty frustrated, but we had to reassemble the compressor with a new bearing and get it running.

"This time, we were ready. The whole team stayed around for the restart and watched the vibration readings on start-up. As soon as I saw the spike, we shut it down again. I thought Brian was going to blow a gasket, I mean three shut downs in three days! But he hung in there with us. This time when we got down to the bearing we saw something different. There was a frosting on the bearing which had clearly come from a static charge. Apparently a charge was building up on the shaft and arcing over to the bearing. The charge was causing the pitting. We would never have found it if we had not been so set on finding the source. We were willing to sacrifice the short term for the long term. And the best part is the fix.

"It turns out there used to be a guy in maintenance who checked all of the static brushes on equipment, but he retired last year. The spring that holds the brushes to the shaft was shot and was allowing a charge to build. The fix was less than ten cents. The spring is now on our standard operator PM checklist. We also alerted all of the operating teams with similar equipment to check for this defect. We went back and found twenty-five failures with almost $500,000 in cost in the last twelve months due to failures from this problem."

The whole Action Forum group gave Chuck and his team a standing ovation, as Chuck beamed with pride.

"That was quite an action team," James beamed, as he walked up and shook Chuck's hand. "Thank you all for your efforts and commitment, and thanks to you, Brian, for your leadership," James added as he shook Brian's hand while he clapped him on the back.

James pulled out a sheet of "no bug" hardhat stickers and gave one to each team member, explaining how each person who reports an eliminated defect in the future would also receive one.

"You'll notice that yours is a bit different in that the bug is gold colored. We are reserving those for action teams that can show a value of $500,000 or more. Now every defect is important, mind you, but we want to recognize when a team makes such a significant contribution."

The team all seemed genuinely appreciative of the recognition. James had debated bigger awards with Chance and the shadow network, but the consensus was that, if they had the hundreds of teams they anticipated, the cost to reward each would be prohibitive. And if they only awarded the high value teams, then people would spend too much time looking for larger problems, completely overlooking the hundreds of lower value defects that were out there. There were two additional important factors that had influenced his decision.

First, it could be difficult to determine who exactly contributed. For instance, in Brian's action team, should the supervisor be included in the reward even though he had not been on the team? Or what about the experts who were brought in to diagnose the problem? If they stuck to recognition, they could broadly include all contributors.

The second consideration had been the capper. They were eager to drive ownership and intrinsic interest in defect elimination. A big award meant outside motivation. Some people would be working on teams not because they personally believed in defect elimination, but because they were being artificially motivated. When the award was taken away, as it surely would be at some point, the motivation for those people would go away as well.

The rest of the team presentations went well, and each was recognized for their contribution. At the end of each presentation, James always asked two questions, "What other defects did you turn up in this process that we should be addressing?" and, "What obstacles did you encounter in doing this project that we can work on to get out of your way?" He expected Cindy and the operations supervisors to catalog the answers to the first question, which were often various ways that the same defect that the team focused on could pop up in other parts of the plant. The answers to the second question he recorded himself.

When the action teams were done talking about their results, the Action Forum discussed their views on the obstacles to defect elimination. There was not much consensus. Clearly no one had thought about the topic much so James decided to collect the list of issues and wait until the next forum to see if a pattern emerged, then he could take action. Finally, each of the supervisors discussed their top ten defects and which of these defects they wanted to pursue. Cindy chimed in with some recommendations as well, and they quickly had a list of thirty new topics for the following month. James then asked each of the supervisors to schedule a time with Cindy, and the head of personnel, who had a database of all of the previous teams, and the current assessment of who the real "go-getters" were. They would put together a team that could tackle the problem and have the best chance of "infecting" some additional "go getters".

After the first Action Forum was adjourned, James sat in his office with the door closed and mentally reviewed the forum. Overall, James was pleased. He was happy with the design of the stickers the marketing department had created. If the reaction of the action team members was any indication, the stickers were a really brilliant idea.

Over the next few weeks, James fell into a routine of reviewing action teams every Thursday with his staff. The entire group of managers had taken to wearing golf shirts to the plant everyday that had pocket emblems of a bug with a line through it "Ghostbusters" style. Visitors often made fun of them for dressing alike, but there was certainly no doubt in anyone's mind that they were aligned and that each of their priorities was defect elimination.

Costs were dropping like a rock. The plant was quickly shedding a lot of the outside vendors they normally called in to do repair work. Steve was working on training the mechanics to take on some of the irregular and overhaul work they normally farmed out, in order to make further cuts. Steve had even transitioned three guys out of tech roles to work on planned maintenance tasks. Two became planners and one an inspector. Unlike the last time, when James had had to expand headcount and cost to get those functions, this time he was able to fund it with resources freed up from the elimination of unplanned work.

While James could not guarantee that there would be no forced cuts, he was very committed to getting all of the savings he could out of overtime reduction, outside services, and natural attrition, before he considered any cuts. Atlanta was a vibrant job market, and they had always struggled to hold good people given all of the other options, so James was hoping to avoid any big cuts. It was a bit of a paradox for James, why all of the hourly workers were so committed to a process that was eliminating their overtime.

One day after an action team session, James stopped an old buddy in the hall. He was from the Extrusion line and one of the first operators to join the shadow network. After thanking him for his work on the latest action team, James asked the question that he'd been curious about. He knew his old buddy would give him an honest answer. "I've seen the overtime figures for your line. They're way down. It seems like all this defect elimination stuff has really cut it back. What do your guys think about that? Is it a big negative?"

The operator thought about it for a moment and then replied, "You know, different people feel differently about overtime. There's definitely a group who feel entitled to it. They feel like it is a part of the job and that they need it. There are others who would just as soon be home with their families. But I have to say, I never thought about it much in regards to defect elimination. I mean, really, it just makes sense. It's no fun coming into a place where you know everything is going to be screwed up, and you're just going to be working on the same stupid problems day after day. It's nice to finally be in control. You know, James, we've known all of this for a long time. We're all just happy you managers are finally on board." With that, he laughed out loud and slapped James on the shoulder.

James had to chuckle to himself as he heard his old buddy's laughter echoing in the halls as he walked away.

By the third Action Forum session, things were beginning to get routine. The action teams with the largest impact, the most commitment, or the biggest potential for learning, were invited to the monthly sessions. The rest came to the weekly Thursday sessions with James, Steve and Buzz.

In the meeting, they discussed how Jennings had requested they add planning into the corporate reports. Fortunately, they were already tracking that number in the scorecard so they were on top of that aspect. They had a discussion about how Jennings obviously believed that the leading indicator was planned maintenance work, but they knew differently. They discussed their belief that ownership was the leading indicator, and that good planning was a consequence of good defect elimination.

They then moved on to action teams. Results were reported, and they spent a few minutes discussing obstacles and letting the management team know about other defects that they had encountered. In the session, Steve took the middle part of the agenda to talk about obstacles. They had now heard from over one hundred successful action teams between the Action Forum and the Thursday reviews. Additionally, Cindy was continuing to follow up with the teams that petered out. Steve took the floor to share some of his findings on the main obstacles.

"Okay, based on all of the teams we have heard from, including the incomplete teams that Cindy has talked about, we seem to have obstacles that fall broadly into three buckets.

"First, there is a general problem with funding. Many teams feel that the formal process they have to use for getting funding for defect elimination is too cumbersome and requires too much justification. There are too many people who can say 'no'. Also, there are many managers who are frustrated because you, Buzz, and I are over-ruling them after they've already said 'No'.

"Second, teams feel that there is an obstacle regarding ownership. They feel pressured to work on specific teams from this forum when they know about other defects they think would be easier to solve or have more impact for them personally. There also seems to be a belief that we are being a governor on the process, and people would do more if they didn't feel the need to be involved in such a formal process. They feel good about the forum and the Thursday sessions, but they feel that the high profile nature of it, along with our participation, makes the bar too high for fancy presentations and 'impress the boss' stuff. Several have commented that they spent more time preparing for their presentation than eliminating the defect.

"Finally, we seem to lack really strong electrical and computer expertise. A large percentage of our team failures are on defects that require this expertise. The teams are simply not able to find the proper experts to help solve the root cause of their problems," Steve concluded, sitting back in his chair.

"Interesting," James responded, as he tapped his fingers on the table processing the information Steve had reported. "Do you have any thoughts on what we should do?"

"Well, on the third point, I agree we do have an issue. I'd like to get two of our electrical techs to go through some advanced sensor training and a host of computer training sessions. Also, we have one tech retiring at the end of next month. I'd like to hire a replacement who is a real computer expert," Steve replied.

One of the supervisors jumped in, "You know, it would also help if we did two things for the operators. One, we need to get them some basic training on computers and electronics so they can do a better job of diagnosing the problem. I see the work orders that go over to maintenance, and the descriptions are usually helpful things like 'computer broke' or 'system hung'. We should be able to do better than that. Second, the environment we put these computer systems in cannot be ideal. There is so much dust and, in some cases, heat. I think we ought to put an action team on that topic and see what they come up with."

"Both great ideas," replied James. James turned to Buzz and said, "Buzz, I assume you have the skill issues?" James then turned to Cindy, "Can we add the computer environmental defects to the team list for next month?" Cindy nodded her head as she was writing, acknowledging that she already had it on the list.

Steve picked back up on the conversation, "As far as the funding issue goes, I have given it some thought, and while I think it could be dangerous, I want to discuss freeing up some money to support the teams. I think we should set a limit, but if teams need funds, they can tap this money by sending a simple request to accounting. No justifications, no presentations, no decision makers to say no. The only requirement is that their team needs to be in Cindy's database. What do you guys think?" Steve asked looking around the table.

The answer was clear from the body language James picked up on as he scanned the group for their reactions to Steve's idea. James really wasn't surprised. After all, sitting around the room were those that normally approved fund requests. James knew exactly what they were thinking. If their grimaces and tense postures were any indication, they were obviously wondering how they would keep control of their departments if teams could get funding for any idea without their approval. James kept quiet to see how it would play out as one of the maintenance supervisors finally spoke up.

"Steve, I understand where you're coming from, and I want to make it easier on the teams, too. But if they're allowed to make investments with no oversight, how do we know that we're focused on the right priorities? Isn't it management's job to decide these things?"

An operations supervisor chimed in, "And how will we know if teams follow proper engineering change request protocol? We don't want to create safety issues."

Buzz interjected, "Yeah, what if people go crazy, and we have millions of dollars in added expenses for dubious projects? How would we be able to stop that?"

It seemed the concept was sinking fast. James had his view, but he wanted to give the team a chance to talk through the issues before he took control.

Then one of the engineers spoke up, "Look, in the end we're approving something like 90% of the requests that come up through the chain. The average team so far has spent a whopping $1,100, and the average is deceptive. Almost 70% of the teams so far have not used a dime. They've made their changes with no cost or found a way to fold that cost into normal operations. All of the things you are bringing up could be issues but, to date, they simply haven't been. We are well on our way to having two hundred teams complete. I really think the teams have earned the trust to be responsible with the funds."

James decided that it was a good time to share his thoughts. "Let me see if I can sum up some of the concerns and address a few with a solution," James interjected.

"First, I hear concerns on the overall amount this could lead to. I doubt that will be an issue, but to take it off the table let's set a cap at five hundred thousand dollars for the year. We'll let people know about the cap so they feel some obligation to leave funds for their peers. As Steve said, there should absolutely be a limit on the amount per project. Based on the team figures from engineering, I think five thousand dollars is a good place to start. There have been only a handful of teams that might have an issue with that limit. Those teams can still use the formal process for requesting funds. Steve, I assume you can allocate the budget within maintenance and put in place the simple request process?"

When Steve nodded in affirmation, James continued.

"Second, I hear concerns about following standard procedures. We can't leave all standard procedures in place. That would defeat the purpose of what Steve has proposed. But I agree that we cannot violate engineering change order rules for safety reasons. I suggest we create a short training course on those procedures so teams know their boundaries and when to call in help. Cindy, I would like you to set up a ready contact person who would be the on-call person for teams when they need help."

James continued when he noted Cindy had finished writing on her note pad, "Finally, I hear a lot of concerns about control. Frankly, I'm feeling those concerns myself. We've not even gotten to the second issue yet, but it is becoming quite clear that we are the bottleneck in defect elimination. We can only keep the control we have if we are willing to go slower. Guys, I don't think we can afford to go slower. We are all going to have to get comfortable giving up some control."

It was obvious to James that not everyone was in complete agreement with his plan, but they kept their reservations to themselves, and a fair number were nodding their heads in agreement, so James was satisfied on that point.

"Well, let's discuss what control you are willing to give up," stated one of the operations supervisors. "Can we discuss the second issue? I have to say that I agree with the assessment. Why do you guys need to review every action team on Thursdays? Don't you think by now we know the routine, and which teams to recognize and which to push harder? I've heard that you are now restricting each team to five minutes, and not spending any time thinking about how to apply the lessons they learned more broadly, or to investigate what other defects they encountered. As I sit through these sessions, that seems like one of the most valuable parts.

Maybe you guys should give the reviews and the recognition to us. If there is something we need help with or want you to know about, we'll bring it to this session monthly."

"Yeah," added another supervisor, "I have to agree, and also, we really don't need you picking our action teams. The guys in the field can do that on their own just fine. It just adds a step, and frankly, there really are some people who think they have to wait for our permission to start a team. That's just crazy. I think you ought to trust us to launch the teams in our own areas. We can keep working with Cindy and HR to make sure that we are incorporating the best ideas and driving ownership, but we don't need to do that in a formal setting."

James mentally cringed. After all, this defect elimination focus was his baby. He had bet his career on it, and if he was being honest with himself, he really liked being in the middle of all the teams and hearing the war stories. Now they were telling him to butt out, and that was a bitter pill to swallow. He listened to the rest of the feedback, and after taking a deep breath, responded with what he knew to be the correct decision, as much as it pained him to make it.

"I have to admit, I've felt compelled to hold on to control of the action teams. I just felt that if I made it clear what a priority it was to me personally, I'd get better buy-in. But I see your point of view, at some point it feels like a lack of trust, and logistically it becomes a choke point. So starting next week, we'll cancel the Thursday reviews, and you guys can take over. We'll also quit deciding action teams in this forum, and you guys can make those decisions within your areas, effective immediately. I would like to have a quick review of them each month just to make sure we're all aligned, and no major topic is going unaddressed. Will that work for you all?"

James was gratified to see every head in the room nodding their agreement, which reinforced the fact that he'd made the right decision. "Great, so with that decision made, I think we're all done here today." As everyone got up to leave, James sat back in his chair and watched them file out of the room. He contemplated everything they'd discussed that day. He knew that by the end of the meeting, he had effectively placed his initiative, and his own fate, in the hands of his employees.

A week later, James was thrilled to discover that he had no reason to worry. The new roles and funding for action teams caused the defect elimination activity to explode. That Monday, Cindy reported that thirty new action teams had been formed and reported in to her. Apparently, they really had been the bottleneck. It was not just idle griping.

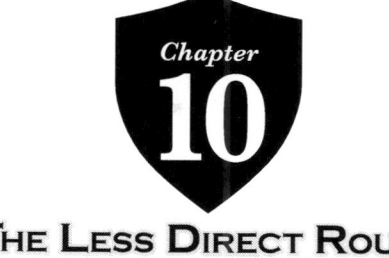

The Less Direct Route

James kicked back in his recliner at home, watching TV with his family. The plant controller had dropped off the plant's latest scorecard earlier that evening, and although he had been itching to go over it, he'd decided to wait until the kids were up in bed, and Carol had her nose planted firmly in her latest novel. Carol had really been putting pressure on James to focus more on the family, and it was a bone of contention between them.

When the house was quiet, and James finally had the opportunity to retreat to his office to go over the scorecard, he was shocked at the numbers.

Atlanta Scorecard 6: June 12th			
Key Performance Indicator	**Description**	**Atlanta Plant Current Year Forecast**	**Best in Class**
Maintenance as a % of Replacement Value	Maintenance cost, excluding capital compared to the estimated capital cost to replace the plant equipment	3.4%	2%
Overtime %	Percent of overtime for hourly workers	17%	<5%
Waste cost as a percent of raw materials cost	The cost of all scrap and defective output compared to total input	1.4%	0.2%
Raw material cost per ton of output	Applied only to plants making similar outputs	$19.18	$20
Labor cost per ton of output	Applied only to plants making similar outputs	$10.61	$7.30
Consumables, parts and outside repairs cost per ton		$4.01	$2.50
Energy costs per ton		$7.40	$7.25
% Planned Maintenance Work	% of work that is planned and scheduled at least 1 week in advance	74%	95%
Production % of Max	Maximum production the plant can operate at	85%	98%
Earnings	Last 12 months earnings in millions of dollars	$4.6 million (profit)	$40 million (profit)
Recordable injuries/ 200K man hours		0.78	<0.50
Ownership	Employees actively look for ways to improve the plant	100%	>60%

The turnaround was nothing short of miraculous. Every metric had improved. They still had a way to go to get to the 20% cost target, but it now seemed achievable. He had to admit, he was extremely proud of the "ownership" number. The fact that they were now profitable was impressive, and he knew that this was his salvation as a plant manager. James was racking his brain trying to remember the last time he needed to intervene to solve an equipment problem or respond to a customer about an unplanned outage. It just didn't happen these days.

They were now making 4.6 million dollars per year as opposed to a loss of 4.1 million dollars when they started the defect elimination program. They didn't have to go through a worse before better experience like they had with the MRS program. James concluded that this was most likely due to the fact that the pilot activities that led to defect elimination were started while they were still doing the MRS program. The lagging indicator, earnings, had finally come around. There were four other lagging indicators that had not reached their goals, but the momentum was headed in the right direction, and being profitable, he knew, would give them the time they needed to bring the other indicators along. Specifically, he was most concerned about the safety performance.

As James sat there admiring his numbers with a grin pasted to his face, he noticed there was a second page attached. The controller had attached the planned maintenance scorecard that Jennings had requested.

James looked at the numbers in disbelief. The percent of planned work had skyrocketed. He wondered why. They weren't even working on planned maintenance right now. When they had originally started with MRS, they had struggled to get to 72% planned work before dropping back to 20%. If these numbers were right, they were now at 74%. He was shocked. He would have to get to the bottom of this, something just didn't seem right. He anxiously fired off an e-mail to Steve and the controller, knowing he wouldn't sleep well that night.

The following morning he pulled together the controller, Steve, and Buzz, to get to the bottom of the numbers. He could not have the report go out to Jennings and his peers if the numbers were wrong. He would be crucified since he was notoriously known as the plant manager who killed the planned maintenance program.

The controller explained, "So, I pulled the base numbers and as best as I can figure, James, there is no mistake with the numbers. We *are* at 74% planned work."

"Right, but it's interesting how we got there. This month we have almost the exact same number of planned jobs completed as last year…" Steve started.

"Then the numbers *can't* be right," James interrupted.

"You didn't let me finish. Every percent has a numerator and a denominator. Remember, the base is total jobs. Well, we've cut the reactive work so much that even with only marginal improvements in planning, our percentage has increased significantly. The numbers are correct, James!" Steve shot back.

"Incredible! When I think about all those months that we spent banging our heads against the wall with that MRS program, and how it destroyed both Buzz's and my relationship with Vance…" James stopped mid-sentence, "…incredible. Who would have ever guessed?"

"Chance, that's who," Steve replied as he left James' office.

James sent his scorecard up to Chance by e-mail later that morning and rang him around lunch time. "Pretty amazing numbers, huh?" James asked.

"This is exactly what I've come to expect from you," Chance replied. "I just pulled together the numbers for all the plants. It looks like you're going to be number two behind St. Louis on the planned maintenance benchmark. That ought to raise some eyebrows." Chance shifted to a mock interviewer's voice, "Please tell us James, how did your plant achieve such a high level of planning? It must have been quite some effort."

"No," said James playing along with the joke, "we listened to the advice of a good friend and took the easier road through the valley." They both laughed out loud.

James' laughter died down as he asked, "In all seriousness, though, I do have a question. Looking at the numbers, I still don't see how I'm going to get the cost structure that St. Louis has. Am I missing something here?"

"Yes, you are," Chance chuckled. "Remember, James, your cost issue is mostly a denominator issue. Your costs are spread over too low of a volume. You've done a phenomenal job getting the plant running better and the costs down, but you have to engage sales and marketing. Let them know that you're open for business and looking for volume."

"You're right," James agreed. "We really have a lot of extra capacity now. I've been using it for extra down time to let the teams work on defects, but we need to sell out that capacity now."

James and Chance finished up their conversation and promised to talk again at Jennings' follow-up benchmarking meeting that was just around the corner. James didn't even bother to put down the phone. He simply pushed the disconnect button and dialed the VP of sales for his division, Janet Stevens.

When Janet picked up the phone, James started with the usual greeting he used when calling any of his sales guys, "I didn't pull you away from an important golf game did I?" James asked sarcastically.

"Ha, Ha," Janet replied. "If you grease monkeys could just make the stuff right, we wouldn't have to go out and purposely lose at golf to these customers to make up for it," she shot back in jest.

"Yeah, right," James replied. "Janet, I called because I need to sell out some capacity. Is there any business that we can go after together?"

"They don't let you out much there, do they, James? We're way ahead of you. All my sales staff has been down in the trenches the last nine months going through the Defect Elimination Game along with your people, and half of them have already been on an action team. You know, the creation of The Defect Elimination game was just brilliant, and the employees are getting so much out of it. We owe all these benefits we're realizing to the game, and now we're about to ink a deal for you guys based on one of those teams.

"It seems the conversation got started when the team asked my sales guy about defects. Like any good salesman, he let them know he didn't know a thing about how the product was produced, but he did know that he couldn't sell a specialty product that couldn't reliably hit the higher specifications. Then he told them that there was major specialty business out there if they could hit the spec. That action team, created in a workshop, ended up spawning two more action teams and damned if those guys aren't hitting the spec. We just went out and sold the business.

"I tell you what, James, next time we'll let you know somewhere in the middle that we're growing your business for you, so you won't be so surprised," Janet informed him.

"Alright, then," James said. "Next time can you have my request done six months ahead of my asking for it instead of this measly three months? Seriously though, keep it up. We have some fairly serious capacity opening up."

"Will do, James. You keep them hopping down there. We're hearing nothing but great things from our customers."

James was satisfied as he said goodbye and hung up the phone.

Over the next several weeks, James saw dramatic acceleration in the performance improvement of the plant. Pushing responsibility for the teams out to the supervisors had been a huge hit. Not only had it accelerated the pace of teams, since he and his staff were no longer the bottleneck, but it had really helped with the buy-in from the supervisors who had, as a group, always seemed a bit reluctant.

It still made James uncomfortable at times not to be involved with the team selection and report outs. He would see some of the topics and cringe because they were not topics he would have prioritized, but he now knew that to unleash the power of his organization, he had to let go of the reins a bit. There was no way to engage the entire organization, foster the kind of real ownership he was trying to encourage, and maintain tight control. And yet, he thought if he had turned over control before defect elimination, when the vision was less clear, it would have been a train wreck.

Ownership worked at his site because almost everyone held a common vision of what they were trying to accomplish. They knew what the objective was, and they all knew how they intended to get there. Without that, empowerment would have just led to chaos. The Defect Elimination Game had helped create that common purpose and vision. The teams had helped, and the shadow network and Action Forum also played key roles in creating the right culture. James wondered how else he could explain an organization that anticipates excess capacity and improves the process on its own in a way that allows the sell-out of that capacity without any prompting from senior management.

The additional volume also helped tremendously. In addition to the financial support it gave the site, James found there was a lot of pride mixed in with winning new business that they had not been capable of running before. On top of that, the extra demand gave a new sense of urgency to the reliability efforts. James had felt a lull in the pace of the initiative as the site got closer to its goals. The added demand fired everyone up again and got them focused on taking out the next level of defects.

Three weeks later, James left the house with the suitcase he had packed the night before. His plan was to get a few hours in at the office, and then catch a mid-afternoon flight up to headquarters. A dinner was planned for all of the plant managers, and then another all-day session the following day. It had been a year since the cost challenge had been thrown down, and Jennings wanted to make sure everything was on track.

When James arrived at the hotel for dinner, he headed to the bar area where he noticed several small groups of his peers standing around talking and having a few cocktails. He walked up to the bar and ordered a drink. As it was being made he looked around for Chance. The bar tender slid him his drink. James thanked him as he picked it up and began a circuit of the room to continue his search for Chance, periodically stopping to chat with his peers. In the middle of one conversation, James felt a hand on his shoulder.

"Long time no see, stranger," a booming voice greeted him as he spun around to see the outstretched hand of his former consultant, Robert. James smiled in greeting and shook his hand earnestly as they exchanged trivialities. After a few moments of polite talk, Robert casually maneuvered James away from the group he had been talking with.

"James, Jennings gave me a preview of the benchmark rankings this afternoon. I have to admit, I was a bit stunned to see you guys at the top of the heap on planned maintenance. I guess the work we did there paid off more than you expected."

Not wanting to go into a lot of detail or hurt Robert's feelings, James simply responded, "Uh, yeah. You guys did some great work."

"Oh, come on, that's a bit weak given the turn around at your site. It seems you kicked us out just as things were about to turn. I told you we were right on the verge of something big. You guys should let me come in and write it up as a success story for us. The other plants could really learn something from what you've done."

James tried to hold back a smirk as he thought that Robert might not be too happy if the other plants learned the real truth behind what he had done. He decided to take the high road and responded vaguely, "Well, why don't you call me some time and maybe you can come in to see what we've accomplished."

Jennings' assistant then entered the room and asked everyone to come in and be seated for dinner. James entered the dining area and found himself seated at a table between Jennings and Chance, who must have sneaked in after the cocktail hour.

The conversation over dinner ranged from politics to problems in the industry. James had to admit he was enjoying himself. With his plant performing well, he didn't feel the pressure he normally felt when he was around Jennings. For the first time, he felt like part of the inner circle.

They were joking about some mutual friends who were in corporate roles when Chance looked over at James and said, "James, maybe you should come to Corporate and apply what we've both learned at a corporate level for all the plants."

James noticed Chance and Jennings exchange a quick, furtive glance, but before he could ponder the significance of the look, someone on the other side of the table engaged Jennings with a question on a different topic.

Relieved that Jennings' attention had been diverted, James whispered to Chance under his breath, "Jeez, Chance, bite your tongue would you. I've just settled the plant into the Precision Domain. The last thing I need is a new assignment."

Chance chuckled as he applied himself to his dessert without further comment.

The following day, James breezed through the meetings. Jennings had seated everyone according to performance again. This time James was in the second row. Everyone was astounded that the Atlanta site could have moved up so rapidly.

One plant manager jokingly bellowed, "I know what I had to do just to move up two spots. What did *you* do James? Lay off the whole plant?"

James laughed out loud, along with everyone else.

The rest of the day was spent in information sharing sessions. James listened to one presentation after another. They all outlined how they were cutting programs that James considered to be essential. Many plants deferred maintenance. A host of other desperate measures had been taken.

One of his peers outlined how they raised the temperature on the plant floor by eight degrees to save on air conditioning costs, which in James' opinion had to take a toll on the workers. James looked around after that particular presentation wondering if anyone else shared the same concerns, but every face in the crowd displayed the same appropriate look of interest and attentiveness.

Several went on to explain how they were in the middle of implementations with MRS but complained bitterly about the added costs and distractions and wondered when the payoff would appear.

With the exception of the St. Louis plant, he heard all top-down mandated changes and none that involved engagement of the workers.

When it was James' turn, he stood and set up graphs of his scorecard measures over the last year. He said nothing for a moment, giving everyone a chance to view each of the graphs and allowing the magnitude of the improvement to sink in before he began.

He put up a slide with just three words on it: "What - Defect Elimination". He spent about ten minutes explaining what he meant by the term "defects", where defects come from, and what problems they cause.

He then put up his second slide with just two words: "How - Ownership". James talked about creating a shared vision, inspiring people to look for defects, and giving them a platform to take action. He talked about not getting in people's way and giving them the resources to get their work done. He also shared a couple of real life examples.

Finally he put up his last slide, again with just two words: "Who - Everyone". James talked about The Defect Elimination Game workshops and the teams that were created in them. He told the plant managers about all the outsiders that were involved and how much they contributed. He ended his presentation with a recap on the statistics in the number of teams launched, defects eliminated, and savings realized.

When he finished, he sat down and noticed that his peers were obviously dumbfounded. Chance and the St. Louis plant manager simply sat in their seats and nodded quietly to one another.

In the break that followed his presentation, James was inundated with questions. He repeated large portions of his presentation and promised to send more detailed information to many. It was amusing to him that he received all of the questions when the St. Louis plant had sustained this type of performance for years. He guessed that most of his peers were like him and had chalked up the St. Louis Plant's performance to some freaky phenomenon that they could never fully understand or replicate. But here in front of them was a mere mortal that had taken one of the laughing stock facilities and turned it around. James felt good, really, really good.

When James got pulled out for his one-on-one with Jennings, it was a completely different meeting from last year. Jennings was all sunshine and light. He did tell James not to let the success go to his head and to make sure he met his final cost numbers.

"I take it your presentation went well? You guys sure have made a difference down there. Hey, let me ask you a question. Everyone is complaining about the MRS initiative, but Robert keeps telling me that it was essential to your success down in Atlanta. What do you think we should do with the planning initiative?"

"Well, Jennings, if you have just a minute, I can tell you a story about a man who lived in a valley…"

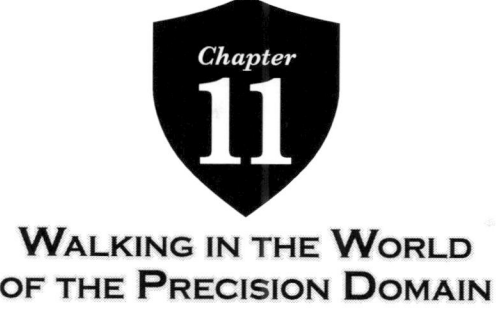

Chapter 11

WALKING IN THE WORLD OF THE PRECISION DOMAIN

Almost two years after that fateful accident that had set the wheels of change in motion, James was listening to the radio on his way in to work. The change at the Atlanta plant had been remarkable. It was hard to remember the old days clearly, but the reactive mode of operating the plant had been painful. As a team, they had taken a site that seemingly could do no right, and transformed it into a world leader. The deadline to hit the CEO's aggressive cost reduction targets had come and gone. Although Atlanta was doing extremely well and improving in areas, they had not met all of the targets. As the additional volume kicked in, all of the allocated costs dropped like a rock on a per ton basis. There was still work to be done, but they were currently making a nice profit.

Atlanta Scorecard 7: September 1st			
Key Performance Indicator	Description	Atlanta Plant Current Year Forecast	Best in Class
Maintenance as a % of Replacement Value	Maintenance cost, excluding capital compared to the estimated capital cost to replace the plant equipment	2.7%	2%
Overtime %	Percent of overtime for hourly workers	10%	<5%
Waste cost as a percent of raw materials cost	The cost of all scrap and defective output compared to total input	1.2%	0.2%
Raw material cost per ton of output	Applied only to plants making similar outputs	$19.27	$20
Labor cost per ton of output	Applied only to plants making similar outputs	$8.88	$7.30
Consumables, parts and outside repairs cost per ton		$2.46	$2.50
Energy costs per ton		$7.30	$7.25
% Planned Maintenance Work	% of work that is planned and scheduled at least 1 week in advance	89%	95%
Production % of Max	Maximum production the plant can operate at	90%	98%
Earnings	Last 12 months earnings in millions of dollars	$17.5 million (profit)	$40 million (profit)
Recordable injuries/ 200K man hours		0.54	<0.50
Ownership	Employees actively look for ways to improve the plant	100%	>60%

His mind wandered to his latest challenge. Based on their performance over the last year, they had vaulted in ROIC over the rest of the plants and had won a major expansion.

James was working with engineering to get the new lines designed as defect-free as possible. He had seen firsthand that design defects were among the toughest to deal with and often could only be abated, not completely eliminated. He wanted to make sure that as few defects as possible made it into the new units. He had action teams working with the engineers on the designs to make sure that any known defects in the old equipment, as well as any they could anticipate, were eliminated before construction began. It was great to have time to spend on positive issues rather than reacting to the issue of the day.

After arriving at work, James checked in with several of the operators and ended up spending more time socializing than he had planned. He glanced at his watch and realized he was running late. By the time he made it to his office, he was ten minutes late for his scheduled call with Chance. He hurried to his desk and picked up the phone to dial Chance's number. When Chance answered on the first ring, he shot out a boisterous greeting.

"Hey there, James, thought you might have forgotten about me."

James laughed out loud and replied, "Not likely. I walked around the plant this morning and things are so quiet, in comparison to last year, I can hardly believe it. The infighting is gone, and the reactive emergencies are gone. It's almost a little boring around here. Thank goodness for the expansion. It's helping to keep everyone on their toes," James chuckled.

"Well, I'm still not sure the engineers here at Corporate have bought into the whole defect elimination culture. You know, all of their metrics are simply on-time, on-budget. They never seem to remember that less than 20% of the cost is in the original installation, and over 80% is in the imbedded costs based on decisions made in the installation," Chance added.

"Don't worry. My guys simply won't accept defects around here anymore. They'll keep sending it back until they get it right," James said confidently.

"...And you know what else?" James added, continuing before Chance could answer, "I was going through some of my old notes earlier, and I found my list of top five priorities that I had made back when I took over as plant manager. Do you remember the discussion we had about that?"

"That's right, I do remember that," Chance replied. "Let me see if I remember them correctly. Get the plant capacity up, improve on-time and on-schedule deliveries, reduce operating expenses and get closer to a world class safety performance? Am I right?"

James chuckled, "Yeah, you got the goals right but you forgot one."

"Yeah? Which one?"

"Become the choice within the company for new capital investment, remember?"

"Ah, that's right," Chance replied.

"But my goals were much more specific than that. I wanted the plant to hit at least 85% of its rated capacity. We've done that. We've hit 100% on-time on-schedule deliveries. The goal was to reduce operating expenses by 10%, and we've improved that by 13%. My team couldn't be more focused or more on track right now."

"You know, James, you're in about the one percent of people in your position able to accomplish those goals. But what about the new people you're bringing in to run the facility? How will you make sure they have the same culture mentality?"

"Well, we decided to take some risks there. The plan calls for hiring them just seven weeks before start-up. I'm going to accelerate that by an additional thirteen weeks and have them work hand in hand with the current team. I can't take a chance on all those inexperienced people adding a bunch of defects. Of course, we'll make sure they all go through a Defect Elimination Game workshop and participate on an action team in their first month, as well. We think that will be enough to get them indoctrinated in the defect elimination culture before they can do any real damage," James explained.

"How about the existing employees? What did you decide to do about tracking teams?" Chance asked.

"The action teams are still going strong," James assured him. "We decided in the Action Forum this month to stop tracking each team. The truth is it is so engrained in the culture now that it was just creating an administrative burden and not helping performance at all. The supervisors still track them, and we'll review them quarterly. It's now part of their formal evaluation. They have to show the defect elimination activity that their team has taken on. And you'll never believe what else we're finally getting implemented!"

James paused for effect, "I've got the team working on getting the CMMS finished. You know that computer system for maintenance. We tabled it over a year ago to work on defect elimination. Now that the workload is so much less, we can really focus on the new elements and not so much on just replicating the old. The truth is that many of the features that we thought were so important a few months ago are minor issues now that we have only 38% of the work orders that we had then. And frankly, now that we have so much of the work going through our inspectors and planners, we need a system that can support them."

"Well, I never thought I'd see the day when you would bring that back," Chance replied.

"It was never the wrong thing to do. It was just the wrong time," James replied.

"You know that I have some mixed feelings about your performance now," Chance informed him sternly.

"Really?" James said in mock seriousness. He knew Chance well enough to guess what his old friend's issue was.

"Yeah, it seems that your scorecard numbers are now beating St. Louis in a number of areas. You got those guys up there pretty fired up. They're not used to looking ahead and seeing another dog leading the pack," Chance teased.

"Well, you just tell them to get used to the view. We have no plans to slow down."

"You know, it was really quite a Hero's Journey," Chance replied. "Now if you recall, we had a deal. I help you with the transformation, and you help me get all of these thoughts organized into something that can be repeated."

"I know, I know," James said running his hand through his hair. "I'll tell you what, before the end of the day, I'll send over a list of the major lessons I learned, and we can start organizing the manual around that."

"Sounds great! I'm going to hold you to it, now," Chance added.

James laughed and said, "No worries, Chance, I've got plenty of time on my hands. I'll talk to you later."

A few weeks later, James was kicking back in his office looking over the completed list he'd sent to Chance. It was late, but Carol and the kids were out of town visiting her parents, so he didn't feel the need to rush home. He thought it was a good list, but he worried if it really captured all of the essential key points that led to his success. After all, he only had the one success. It was hard to know what elements were essential, and he couldn't help but wonder how many critical things may have happened that he never even noticed. Plus, Chance was adding a lot to the manual himself from his own experiences, and from some of the experts he found at DuPont and other places that were practicing defect elimination.

> **Subject:** Lessons Learned
>
> **What to work on:**
> - Focus on defect elimination (all 7 sources, but especially mechanic and operator practices which are primary drivers, and a large source of total defects initially).
>
> **How to get it done:**
> - Engage the entire organization and focus on bottom-up first.
> - Use small, focused, front-line teams that have clear goals and short timeframes to accomplish their missions.
> - Engage the operators in small PMs that catch defects early on.
> - Include outsiders to help challenge old ways of thinking.
>
> **Leading the effort:**
> - Do not make reliability a maintenance issue. It is a business issue.
> - Make sure there is an easy way for teams to get funding that is not too cumbersome.
> - Don't get caught up on teams that fail. Use them to learn about systemic road blocks but otherwise ignore them.
>
> **When things get rolling:**
> - Don't let management be a governor on the pace of change.
> - Decentralize authority and decision making.
> - Engage all three types of leaders:
>   1) Executive - to provide vision and funding
>   2) Network - to bring the best ideas
>   3) Operational - to get things done
> - Make sure you have an open forum where issues can be discussed and resolved.
>
> **Tracking success:**
> - Don't confuse the goals and the means. The goals are to satisfy customers, maximize throughput and keep your license to operate. The means will change over time.
> - Measure engagement and ownership of front-line employees, it is a key leading indicator.
>
> **Integrating traditional Planned Domain activities:**
> - When pursuing planned work, eliminate the reactive work first, making the path much smoother.
> - RCM and other top-down defect analyses can be extremely effective, but only if they are action-oriented.
> - Don't automate a broken process. Fix it first and then automate.

James had only one more question in his mind. Because of the plants that were still trying to implement the MRS program, he had not challenged Robert at the last managers' meeting when he claimed credit for contributing to the success at Atlanta, but he was pretty sure that the MRS program had not been responsible, or even necessary, for the success. He opened up his desk drawer and pulled out a file on the history of the improvement programs. He searched for a recent chart on the percent of planned work to remind himself of the sequence of initiatives, and the results they created.

He studied the graph, which included arrows showing the timing of the MRS program and when the defect elimination program began. James noted that the timing on the defect elimination start point coincided with the point at which the MIT guys completed the game and began using it on a large scale to engage the workers. James recognized that the other plants would not have to reinvent the game to use it.

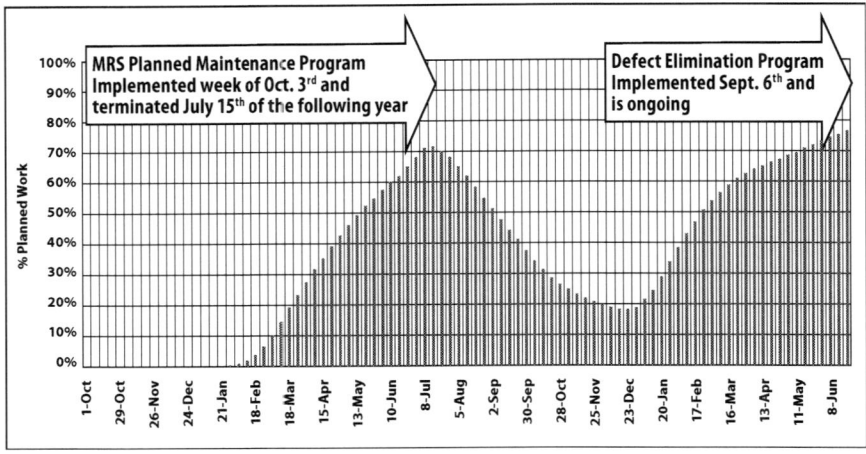

He had to admit that the defect elimination had not yet progressed past the peak of the MRS implementation, so it could simply be a repeat of the last attempt to get to higher levels of planned work. He knew, however, that the level of planned work was progressing much better than the last attempt. No one was complaining about over inspections or excess preventive maintenance. Actually, the reason the planned work was higher was because the total number of work orders were down. He realized it was the old numerator/denominator affect that Chance had pointed out much earlier. The planning was going up because the number of work orders in the denominator was going down. In any event, James couldn't wait to see the latest new score card due to come out soon. It should tell the tale, he thought.

He filed the graph away, and reviewed his list of "Lessons Learned" one last time. He had set up a phone meeting with Chance to go over the material tomorrow. He wanted to go over it in order to make sure he covered everything.

When James called Chance for their scheduled meeting the next afternoon, James was surprised to hear from Chance that Jennings would be joining them. While Jennings had been generally supportive of the concept, he had not personally put any time into it. When Jennings joined the call, James started off the conversation.

"How is the manual coming along, Chance?"

"Great! I should be able to put the finishing touches on the manual this week, which is perfect timing."

"Perfect timing for what?" asked James, hearing both Chance and Jennings laughing out loud. James felt a bit perturbed because he was obviously not in on the joke.

"Well…" Jennings drawled out. "Chance has informed us that he's going to start his retirement week after next. It seems we're short one reliability champion up here at Corporate, and Chance and I sure think you're the right person for the job. It's a nice promotion, James, and as long as you're willing to travel a bit more, you can stay right there in Atlanta."

It was like a bomb had dropped. James gulped twice before answering. He stammered incoherently while he struggled to think of something appropriate to say rather than, "Thanks, but no thanks", which was what he wanted to say. Things were finally under control at the plant. He was now comfortable in his job and confident that he was doing a good job. The idea horrified him as he struggled to think of how to answer.
Chance interrupted James' stammering, "James, the truth is we need you. We need you to take what you've done down there and get the rest of the plants on board."

"Give the offer some thought, and call me with an answer by the end of the week," Jennings said, before he hurriedly signed off the call.

James tried to catch his breath. It was a great promotion, and it showed the tremendous confidence they had in him, but he didn't feel ready to start all over again, especially when things were going so well in Atlanta.

After a long pause, Chance piped in his own opinion, "Look, James, I'm sorry I wasn't able to give you a heads up, but Jennings insisted on handling it this way. You're the perfect person for the position. I would leave feeling so much better knowing that the program was passing to such capable hands."

"Thanks for your vote of confidence, Chance, but I'm just not so sure about all of this," James said with a sigh.

They spent the next hour going over the details and challenges of the job. The more James heard, the more comfortable he became with the idea of working at Corporate.

"Well…," James asked, resigning himself to the position he felt compelled to accept, "…you know what this means, don't you?"

"What's that?" Chance replied.

"Now we have to finish that manual, and quick, because I'm going to need to use it as a tool for helping all the other sites get to the Precision

Domain."

"Well, we are almost finished. It shouldn't be a problem."

"I know, but now I'm thinking that if I'm going to be helping all the other sites to make the same improvements that we have here, I really need a more concrete how-to manual than what we currently have. You know, kind of a detailed recipe for success."

"Well, James, we can certainly make improvements, but after the last bit of information you sent, I think it really is very thorough."

"Well, yeah, I know, but maybe I should have one more meeting with management here and make sure I'm not missing anything. I just want to make sure that what happened here will be easily articulated, and repeated, at each of the other sites. I really need to understand exactly how it happened to do that," James said, as his mind whirled a mile a minute, already trying to mentally go through his schedule to pick a date for the meeting.

Chance laughed out loud and replied, "James, that's exactly why you're the perfect man for this new job. Just let me know how I can help."

"Thanks, Chance, but I just need you here for the brainstorming session I have in mind. I'll let you know the date when I get it all arranged."

"Sure thing, James. I'll talk to you soon."

James said his goodbyes and hung up the phone. He needed to schedule that meeting immediately, but he allowed himself a moment to ponder the changes that were about to happen in his life. He sat back in his chair, staring off into space contemplating the next part of his journey. This time as a weenie from Corporate.

That night after dinner, James dropped the bomb on Carol. He honestly didn't expect her to be enthusiastic about the promotion, but he was surprised by just how vehement her arguments against taking the job were.

"Are you crazy, James? This economy is horrible, and frankly, the position doesn't sound that stable to me. Those kinds of jobs are always the first to go when cutbacks are made. We cannot afford for you to be unemployed. And the goals they'll set will be impossible. They'll be setting you up for failure! And have you even considered how many more hours you'll be working, with the traveling time? Please tell me you are not considering taking this job!"

James grimaced. He'd already made the decision to accept the position, so he knew some fancy footwork was required here. He needed to get Carol's support without making her feel like she didn't have a say at all. He sighed, running a hand through his hair, trying to decide the best course of action.

By the end of the night, they had worked everything out. She was not happy, but he'd appeased her as much as he possibly could, and she'd reluctantly accepted the fact that he would be taking the position.

Two months later, all of the Atlanta managers and supervisors gathered for an informal meeting to discuss details of the Atlanta plant transformation. James wanted to incorporate as many specifics as he could into the manual. They pulled their chairs into a circle in the conference room. James stood at the head of the circle, raising his hands to quiet the room.

"Ladies and gentlemen, as you may know, I've been tasked in my new job with duplicating our successful change effort here in Atlanta at each of the other sites of Modern Products Manufacturing. In order to do that, I've gathered you all here today to discuss the exact chain of events and what you feel are the key elements that made the change effort a success." James looked around the circle, worried at the expressions of disapproval he saw on some faces. "Does anyone have any questions before we begin?" James added, hoping to clear up any questions or concerns anyone might have before he started with the first item on his agenda.

Everyone looked around at each other, before Buzz finally took the lead and spoke up, "Well, James, I guess we're all just a little confused how anything that happened here could be of any help to the other sites. I mean, each site is different. Should we really be helping them out when we compete against them for our numbers?"

The noise level in the room rose as many people nodded in agreement and mumbled to one another.

But Reese's voice carried the loudest, "Yeah, let them figure it all out themselves!" Reese guffawed as the entire room broke out in laughter.

James good-naturedly laughed along with them, but secretly, he was worried. "Well, now, if we can't share our knowledge to help the rest of the company improve along with us, what kind of co-workers would we be? It's about being team players, people."

"Well, I'm just wondering if Modern Products Manufacturing is interested in becoming a learning organization," Cindy piped up. "It certainly never has been that way in the past."

Before James could answer, Buzz jumped in again, "Yeah, they probably wouldn't believe anything we say anyway. It all seems so unbelievable when you see the numbers."

James pulled out the latest report that had been run and passed copies to everyone present. The numbers were amazing. There were a few high-fives as everyone reviewed the report.

"As you can all see, while we haven't achieved all of our goals yet, we've made an incredible improvement in all areas from where we started. Of course, the most important category to me personally is the recordable injuries. We've met our goal for the first time since this all started. These numbers are just too good not to share our knowledge."

James saw everyone looking to each other for approval and after a few nods, they all turned to James again.

Atlanta Scorecard 8: December 15th			
Key Performance Indicator	**Description**	**Atlanta Plant Current Year Forecast**	**Best in Class**
Maintenance as a % of Replacement Value	Maintenance cost, excluding capital compared to the estimated capital cost to replace the plant equipment	2.1%	2%
Overtime %	Percent of overtime for hourly workers	3%	<5%
Waste cost as a percent of raw materials cost	The cost of all scrap and defective output compared to total input	1.1%	0.2%
Raw material cost per ton of output	Applied only to plants making similar outputs	$19.36	$20
Labor cost per ton of output	Applied only to plants making similar outputs	$7.27	$7.30
Consumables, parts and outside repairs cost per ton		$1.05	$2.50
Energy costs per ton		$7.21	$7.25
% Planned Maintenance Work	% of work that is planned and scheduled at least 1 week in advance	100%	95%
Production % of Max	Maximum production the plant can operate at	95%	98%
Earnings	Last 12 months earnings in millions of dollars	$34.5 million (profit)	$40 million (profit)
Recordable injuries/ 200K man hours		0.39	<0.50
Ownership	Employees actively look for ways to improve the plant	100%	>60%

"Now, I realize the numbers are a little hard to believe. But it'll be my pleasure, rather our pleasure, to prove it to them when they realize the same results. We should be proud to share our expertise with our peers." James then looked pointedly at Cindy and added, "And to answer your question, Cindy, Modern Products is committed to becoming a learning organization. That's why they're asking me to take what we've learned here and share it with the other sites." James looked around the circle, noticing everyone was seemingly convinced, or at least finished with their objections.

He nodded and determinedly picked up his clip board with a clean note pad for notes and began in earnest, "Okay, so Cindy, let's start with your work. Tell me what you remember from start to finish. And don't leave anything out."

Cindy walked up to the front of the room, placed a slide on the projector and said, "James, I heard that you were somewhat concerned about the wisdom of doing the MRS program. We can clear that doubt for you right now. Here is the plot of planned work."

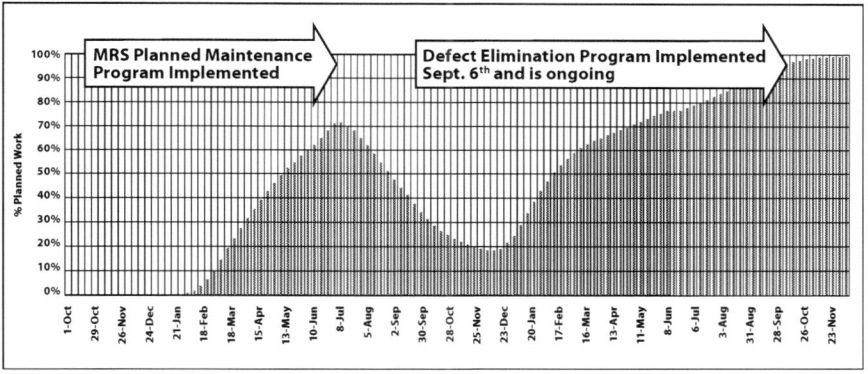

As you can see, there is no question that the planned domain is definitely unstable as we heard from the DuPont guys. As soon as we stopped the MRS program, planned maintenance was not sustainable and the percent of planned jobs dropped quickly."

James sat back in his chair with a grin on his face. This was a great start to the retrospective for James, and he learned much in the next two hours from his employees.

A New Challenge

James entered the corporate offices of his company, Modern Products Manufacturing, carrying what he considered to be his new bible, *The Heroic Change Manual*, that he and Chance had finally completed. After the meeting with his managers, he spent countless hours adding all the wisdom, every key detail, and every best practice that his managers had shared. He was brimming with confidence in the manual and in his new role.

Jennings and the others at Corporate were falling all over themselves with regard to the turnaround in Atlanta, and all he had to do was repeat the success at the other plants. Now that he knew and had documented the formula for success, James believed the execution would be pretty straightforward. No more groping around in the dark, or late night calls to Chance. Now he was the expert. It had taken them a great deal of struggling with ups and downs to get to where they were now. He figured he could get all the other plants to the same level in half the time. He was a month into his new job, and it was time to start implementing the company-wide changes everyone was expecting him to make.

Jennings had called one of his "all-hands" meetings for that morning, and all of the plant managers were in town for it. Half of the agenda had been allotted to James to announce the new reliability initiative and to lay out the plans for enactment.

He and Jennings had spent the previous week laying out the strategy. Jennings was more than happy to let James manage the philosophical side, along with the content, he simply wanted to make sure that James was pacing himself and focusing on where he could get the most bang for the buck. Together they had sorted the plants into three separate "buckets" based on performance. For now, they would leave the top two buckets alone and focus on the lowest performing plants, which were Houston, Philadelphia, Lake Charles and Corpus Christi.

At least three of those sites were relatively close together geographically, thought James, dreading all of the upcoming travel. He was mentally prepared for the long travel hours he'd be putting in, and Carol had resigned herself to being a virtual single parent again.

He had added quite a bit of information to *The Heroic Change Manual* to make sure there was an extremely detailed summary to present to the plant managers. Both a philosophical underpinning, and data to support it, backed up every action. He was ready.

The meeting started off, as they often did, with a review of performance. James was happy that he had convinced Jennings to drop the ridiculously juvenile tradition of seating people by their performance. When the review was over, Jennings glanced over at James and introduced him to everyone in the room, even though he was well known to all.

"Now you all know James. In fact, he was sitting right there with you just a short time ago. James and his team in Atlanta did such an amazing job turning that plant around that I have asked James to move into a corporate role with the responsibility of helping each of you repeat, at your own sites, what he accomplished in Atlanta. He's got a couple of hours of material to go through with you, and then he'll have some assignments for you. I want to make it clear to all of you that the execution of the plan James is about to go over is among my top priorities."

James stood up to a rousing ovation from his former peers. With an introduction like that from Jennings, and a warm reception from the people he would be working with, he felt that his assignment was off to a great start.

James spent the next several hours going through his concept of reliability, what the main goals and means were, and the consequences in terms of cost and safety.

The plant manager from Houston, Billy Heard, was the first to ask a question, "I am not sure what you mean when you say cost reduction is not a goal. The hell it isn't. We're putting most of our effort on that."

"Billy, I understand what you're saying," James replied, "but there are lots of ways to cut costs, some good, some not so good. If we treat it as a goal, it's easy to pursue the not so good ideas because they seem like legitimate ways to hit the goal. However, when we focus on eliminating failures, each action is more likely to be right for the long term and also eliminate costs as a consequence."

Billy turned to Jennings and with a very skeptical tone asked, "So you're okay with us not having a cost reduction goal?"

Fortunately, James had just had this argument with Jennings and was hopeful Jennings would back him up with a supportive answer. Billy was a big, burly guy and often surly and moody. He kept a tight rein on the Houston plant, and no one wanted to be on Billy's bad side. James bit his lip and waited for Jennings' response.

"Well, let's be clear. I need you to hit the cost targets you've been given, but I think James is 100% right when he states that you can get there in long term, sustainable ways, or in ways that cannot be sustained. What James is trying to bring to the table is how to sustain these cost cutting measures or changes."

Billy just shrugged off Jennings' reply, and James would bet a hundred bucks that he hadn't heard the last of the issue, but he continued on. He shared his and Chance's beliefs about defects and the data from Atlanta on the sources of defects. This drew a lot of attention, and as he expected, disbelief, particularly the part about 80% of defects being caused by poor work habits.

The plant manager at the Philadelphia plant, Cheryl Demry, was the first to object. "I don't buy it. No way are my people that sloppy. They are not *accidentally* causing 80% of my problems."

Billy jumped in to add his two cents, "On top of that, this seems to suggest that we could somehow eliminate 80% of the failures and work load. That seems a bit naïve, don't you think?"

Several of the plant managers nodded their heads in agreement.

But the plant manager from Lake Charles, Louis Landry, came to James' defense. "Look guys, I come from a company that was a heavy user of 6 Sigma, and I can tell you that what James is saying is true. We have way too much variability in the process, and it doesn't surprise me at all to hear that James and the Atlanta team discovered that 80% was due to poor work practices. That's completely consistent with my experience with 6 Sigma and where we are as a company."

James took the opportunity to jump in, feeling very confident on this point. "I was where you guys are about two years ago, but I'm here to tell you that we eliminated well over half the failures, and work, in Atlanta by systematically attacking these poor work practices. Everything I've seen about the St. Louis plant would indicate they've seen this sort of improvement as well."

Drew Weaver, the plant manager at St. Louis, who typically kept a fairly low profile at corporate meetings, spoke up in agreement with James. "We have very few failures versus the typical plant. The last time we benchmarked it, we were running 1:5. That is, we have on average one failure for every five that the typical plant has."

After a prolonged silence throughout the room, James decided to continue, realizing that no one really wanted to take on both himself and the St. Louis plant manager in this forum, therefore letting the subject drop for the moment.

James moved on to discuss small teams and how they impact defects.

James knew it would be the most controversial part of the discussion, but he was not prepared for how strong that resistance turned out to be. Most people had the same concern. They believed their people, given the opportunity, would work on frivolous things and waste a great deal of money.

Billy was the most critical, "Humph..." Billy interjected loud enough to make James pause, "we tried that stuff when TQM was such a rage. We had quality circles all over the place. We couldn't get a damn thing done in the plant without tripping over a quality team somewhere. And it got us absolutely nowhere. We had one team that spent a month upgrading the toaster in the break room. That concept may work in other cultures, but we learned the hard way that it does not work here."

James mentally grimaced and took a deep breath, trying to stay calm. He had known coming in that he would find few allies, but he was surprised at the outright confrontational remarks. Even the manager at St. Louis looked skeptical, admitting they had moved away from teams a few years back and had not seen a slip in performance. His only supporter was Cheryl from Philadelphia. She was a die-hard believer in small teams and engagement. James was grateful for Cheryl's support, but he thought he'd have support from at least a couple more plant managers. It was not going as James had imagined. He was supposed to be the expert, and they were supposed to soak it all up and implement his plan. He finished the afternoon session with lessons on leadership, but it was clear that he had lost some of them from the very beginning.

At the end of James' presentation, Jennings stood up to thank James and then added, "Look, I understand that the Atlanta approach may not be ideal for every plant, however, the results James saw in Atlanta are incontrovertible. We have asked the four plants with the lowest overall performance to begin this new initiative first. I expect each of you to work with James, to take the best of what he has to offer, and make a program that you both agree will work for your individual site. We've decided the four plants will be Houston, Corpus, Philadelphia, and Lake Charles for the first six month period. Each of the plant managers for those four sites will need to schedule some one-on-one time with James to get started on a plan."

As the meeting broke up, Billy, from the Houston plant, casually walked over to James, but James wasn't fooled by his outward calmness. The tick in his clenched jaw was a dead giveaway. In spite of all of his earlier disagreements in the meeting, James was shocked by Billy's words.

"Why don't you come on down and see us first. I have a great team, and they'll be all over this. We're great at executing initiatives, and I'd like to get started on this as quickly as possible."

James was surprised and frankly, relieved, thinking maybe he'd misjudged Billy. They agreed to start Monday of the following week, making arrangements to spend the week in Houston creating the plan and launching the effort.

By the end of the week, James was pleased that the other three plant managers had also contacted him by phone. The plan was to spend a week at each of the remaining three plants, filling up James' schedule for the entire month.

Early the following Monday morning, James loaded his *Heroic Change Manual* and a number of files into his briefcase, kissed Carol and the kids goodbye, and headed off to Hartsfield airport to catch his flight to Houston. He had previously forwarded copies of the Change Manual to the leadership teams of each of the plants, in hopes that they would have plenty of time to review his plans before they met. He assumed few would read it outright, but hoped they could at least use it as a reference.

When he arrived at the Houston plant, the leadership team was assembled in their largest conference room with the notable exception of the plant manager, Billy. James was informed that Billy had a busy morning but would join them for lunch. James didn't try to conceal his disappointment. After all, he was taking a week to be in Houston, and the least Billy could have done was clear his schedule.

James took an hour to run through the objectives of the program, which he was calling "Defect Elimination Now". The presentation was more or less the same one he had delivered to the plant managers, and many of the points were identical, but this time he was better prepared for the more difficult questions he expected to pop up. He had detailed data to back up his claims on the sources of defects, and concrete examples of the teams that had tackled the defects. He encouraged the Houston team to replicate the defect analysis if they thought their site was different. James was quite sure the results would be similar, if not identical. He now understood how the conclusion that 80% plus of failures were due to poor work practices, and therefore preventable, was counter-intuitive and hard to believe when you were in the reactive mode. Instead of arguing with people, he decided he would have more success if they discovered it for themselves.

As the meeting progressed, James felt that he had won over some converts. The operations manager, Sean Rayburn, seemed to really get it, and the engineering manager was also on board. He thought both could be great allies, but what he most needed was to get Billy on board. The Atlanta turnaround would have never happened without his executive leadership. He was sure of that. As far as James was concerned, not having Billy on board and active in the initiative meant failure.

They spent the better part of the morning mapping out a game plan. James recommended an early set of actions.

"Guys, I would recommend that this week we take an area and start the program on operator PMs that I described. Then I want to spend some time with each of you getting to understand your operational challenges. That should help us identify important defects. Also, on Thursday and Friday, I've scheduled the leadership team to go through The Defect Elimination Game, which I described earlier. We need to invite about twelve of your front-line employees to attend, and we'll form two to three action teams. I think it will help the teams get aligned on the vision and give you a chance to see how it inspires workers and effectively launches teams."

At this last statement, James noticed that the team seemed to shuffle around and sneak furtive glances at one another.

Finally, one of the men spoke up, "Well, James, that sounds fine, but we have a major safety meeting Thursday to kick-off our Behavior Safety Program, and we're all going to have to spend some time this week on our 360° Performance Reviews, which are due next Monday. Plus, we just launched a "Supervisor as Coach" initiative that we'll have to spend some time on or people are going to wonder if we're serious about it."

"We're going to have to fit this in with all the other priorities," added one of the managers.

James ground his teeth in frustration. This is war, he thought to himself. By the end of the meeting, although he'd agreed to delay The Defect Elimination Game session, he had convinced them to keep the other activities that James had suggested.

When lunch rolled around, Billy did indeed join them. He came into the conference room taking charge and greeting everyone loudly.

Raising his hand in the air to get everyone's attention, he announced, "Guys, this initiative is top priority with Jennings so that means it is top priority with us, as well." Billy slapped James on the back and continued, "James here is a real expert, and unlike most people they send us from Corporate, he has actually been successful, so give him your undivided attention."

James ground his teeth and hid his annoyance behind a big smile. He resented the fact that he would now have to go over the entire plan with Billy again, simply because he either could not, or most likely would not, rearrange his schedule and attend the meeting to begin with.

James recapped the morning session over lunch, and the plan of action for the rest of the week, as well as the plan for the following month. He noticed that Billy seemed oddly detached. He wasn't outwardly disagreeing with anything, but he was obviously not engaged either. James decided to push the issue a bit.

"Billy, in Atlanta, we set up a fund and a process to allow action teams to easily finance their own projects, without red tape. They could get up to five thousand dollars to eliminate their defect, with no hassle. It was really critical to a successful outcome."

Billy, in the middle of taking a gulp of his iced tea, set his drink down and gave James a wave of dismissal.

"I don't think we'll need that, James. Our supervisors have authority to spend more than that."

"Well, we didn't have supervisors on every team. That would be way too limiting," James responded.

"Sure, sure, but all of the team members work for a supervisor. The supervisors can decide on funding after they get the team's recommendations," Billy informed him.

"No," James said firmly. "Teams don't *make* recommendations, they *take* action. This is a critical point, Billy," James bit out slowly and succinctly. Obviously he had not communicated this clearly in his recap.

"Right, right, I just meant the supervisor can deal with funding," Billy said dismissively, as he got up and walked over to the refreshment table for a refill of his ice tea.

James reluctantly let it drop, not that he had much choice in the matter, as Billy went on to openly flirt with the administrative assistant who was cleaning up the conference room and stocking drinks while they were breaking. Billy excused himself to take a rest room break. James had been effectively dismissed, and he had a bad feeling that this would be the only time that Billy would be gracing them with his presence.

James spent the rest of the day, and much of the next, working on identifying areas where high frequency defects could be eliminated. He also spent time with Sean getting the basics of the operator PM's ready to roll out to the single area they had chosen. Sean was supportive, as James had guessed he would be, but whenever it came time to make a commitment on action or timing, he would become very reserved and unable to commit.

After a few such instances, James finally asked him directly, "Sean, is there some reason why you can't commit to any of these actions that we're laying out? It's critical that they get started, and I'm not getting a warm and fuzzy feeling here. Are you going to prioritize them as high? Do you have some reservations here?"

"Oh," Sean rushed to reassure him, "it's not that at all. I think what you're bringing in is like a breath of fresh air. We'll absolutely benefit from it, I have no doubt. It's just that we're overloaded with initiatives right now. And I know Billy. He's not going to let me slow those down to get this one done. I'm just going to have to figure out how to fit this in without rocking the boat too much," Sean added sincerely.

James ran a hand through his hair and sighed. "I am not sure it can work like that, Sean. In Atlanta, we were laser focused on this. I don't know if it will work as one of many initiatives. My guess is that it won't."

Since his confidence had been shaken in his first presentation at headquarters, James had decided to keep another notebook of major questions, lessons, and observations, during the roll-out at the plants to help him through the remaining sites. He flipped open his notebook, turned to the section on questions and wrote, "Can defect elimination be implemented as one of many initiatives?" and wrote his assumed answer next to it, "No".

"I hear you, James, but that's just not up to me. Billy is, well…Billy. You need to talk to him about it," Sean flashed a pained smile with a shrug.

James had managed to coerce Billy into adding him to his calendar for a meeting early Wednesday. He entered Billy's office promptly at 7:00 am prepared to get everything off his chest quickly, in anticipation of interruptions.

As he sat down in front of Billy's desk, James jumped right in, ignoring the preliminaries. "Well, we've laid out some plans for 'Defect Elimination Now'. Your team seems extremely capable and they're on board, but they're having trouble committing to action and timelines because they're worried about competing initiatives," James started.

Billy waved a hand in dismissal, "Oh, don't worry about that. They pull that crap every time we add a new initiative. We always find time to get it done."

"Okay, the second concern I have is about funding. While this effort doesn't take a lot, there are some workshops to pay for and team activities to fund. I think you need to set aside around five hundred thousand dollars, but no one on your staff seems to be comfortable making that commitment. They all defer to you," James added.

"Oh, I'm sure it won't cost that much, James. I told you earlier, we'll let the supervisors deal with the team funding. As for workshops, I've been thinking that a plant-wide kick-off will be much more productive. In fact, we're having one tomorrow for behavioral safety. You should come, and we can model it after that. The hourly guys love them. Gets 'em real fired up," Billy winked, knowingly.

James, feeling decidedly uncomfortable with the non-committal answers he was getting, decided to be frank and lay it all out on the line.

"Billy, from my experience, you're just not doing what it takes to be successful. This is not going to work with the approach you're taking." James intended to make clear that he had serious reservations with regard to Billy's participation.

Billy's good-natured, happy-go-lucky routine disappeared in a flash, and James was surprised at the sudden look of defiance on his face.

"I have a lot of years running this place. I think I know what works here and what doesn't. We'll get your initiative done. You don't need to worry about Houston. We're the masters of pulling these things off."

Billy's good-natured smile reappeared just as suddenly as it had disappeared, and he effectively shut down the initiative discussion with a quick change of subject, "Now, how 'bout we go see if we can't rustle us up some donuts and coffee out of the break room? I'm hungry."

After his rather disappointing session with Billy, James spent most of the rest of the day with Sean Rayburn kicking off the operator PM program at one of the lines. When they introduced the program to the operators, one of the more experienced guys started sniffing the air.

"What does this smell like to you boys?" he asked sarcastically, "Flavor of the month or flavor of the week?"

That got a big roar of laughter from the entire group, but Sean jumped in quickly and asked the guys to give James a chance. After the initial skepticism, the concept was received enthusiastically and seemed to be accepted immediately by the front-line workers. They managed to create a shift cut-over checklist by late afternoon, as well as planned checkpoints and adjustments during the shift. It was a bit frustrating trying to get the work done, as several of the participants were called out of the session to participate in either the "Supervisor as Coach" training or the "360° Review Process".

The following day, James spent the entire morning with the head of engineering. They finalized a list of problem areas and potential defects for teams to tackle. James asked that the head of HR come in to help them pair up talents and "go-getters" to make teams for each defect area. Unfortunately, she was tied up all day in the 360° reviews and supervisor training. The engineering manager apologized profusely and assured James that he would follow up with her later to make the teams.

At lunch that day, James attended the kick-off for the Behavioral Safety program. As Billy had indicated, it did not disappoint. There was a huge barbecue pit that the welders had made sitting out behind the back parking lot of the main office, and there seemed to be a whole butcher shop of meat slowly grilling. There was a sound system set up cranking out music and a huge banner that proclaimed "Behavioral Safety – Do it for Life!" Along the perimeter, there were booths set up with different types of food and games, and each had some message or brochure about behavioral safety. It was quite a show. The whole plant had turned out, or at least all who could be spared at any given time. As Billy had predicted, they seemed pretty enthusiastic, but in James' opinion, the enthusiasm was more about the music and food than behavioral safety. James caught sight of Billy across the field and worked his way over.

As James approached, Billy turned to clap James good-naturedly on the back. "Now see, I told you that a kick-off like this really gets them out. You do something like this for Defect Elimination and people will take notice," Billy said proudly.

James tried for a minute to picture the Defect Elimination banner and the booths for eliminating defects but immediately dismissed the idea. Over his dead body! But to Billy he simply said, "We'll see. I'm not at all convinced." Billy gave James a sideways glance, and then turned to talk to an employee who had just walked up.

James wandered over to a couple of operators he had met the previous day while facilitating the operator PM kick-off. "Some spread!" he said, gesturing to the set up.

"Oh yeah, we're the kings of kick-off's here at Houston," the operator replied with a chuckle.

"What do you guys think about behavioral safety? I understand it's quite a change for the front-line," James said attempting to strike up a conversation.

"I really don't know that much about it, yet," the operator replied between alternating bites of a barbecue rib and an ear of corn on a stick. "We've been working on safety for a long time. I'd be surprised if it were really any different."

"But isn't that the point of this whole production, to start the process of changing?" James asked with dismay. Judging by the food on their plates and the decimated stack of rib bones on the table, these guys had been at it for some time.

"Naw, these shindigs are just to introduce the concept."

"Shoot," the other fellow drawled out as he wiped his greasy hands on his coveralls, "sometimes these kick-off parties are the last thing we ever hear about the initiative. Remember that one we had on TPM a year or two ago?" he asked the guy sitting to his right as he elbowed him to get his attention. "All we had was the barbecue. We never heard it mentioned again."

The receiver of the elbow poke shook his head in disagreement, as he paused to swallow what was in his mouth. "Naw," he interjected, "you're thinking of Asset Utilization, that was just the barbecue. TPM hung around for a week or so. Remember, we created all those lists of things that needed fix'n that everyone then ignored."

"Yeah, yeah, that's right! It was Asset Utilization. That little shindig had the luau theme. That roasted pig was something!" he grinned, licking his lips.

James instantly lost any reservations he had about not having a Defect Elimination kick-off. He thanked the guys and walked back to the office, stopping to get a plate of barbecue along the way. After all, it did smell great. Later that day, he wrote in his notebook, "Big kick-offs without substance substitute activity and the appearance of compliance for real commitment."

James spent a great deal of time that afternoon working with the information technology and accounting groups, gathering the data he needed for the plant assessment he was conducting. He also worked with HR to put in place the qualitative survey that he would need for the assessment. They all committed to executing the assessment the following week.

On Friday, James decided he needed to make another attempt to address his concerns head on. He started with Sean and the engineering manager. "Guys, I have some concerns that this is going to work here. You can't treat this as just one of many initiatives. You can't pull it off with no funding. The workers need a clear vision that is well articulated, and backed up with a way for them to take action. If not, this will go absolutely nowhere."

"You're preaching to the choir, James," the engineering manager responded. "Sean and I have been talking about this all week, and we are totally on board, but you have to help us get Billy there. Without him, I doubt we can make this work."

"You bet. I'll try, but I have to admit, I am not too optimistic about converting Billy. I think the best we can hope for is non-interference. To be honest, I'm not sure that's even enough, but realistically that is all we are likely to get. You guys are going to have to drive it if he agrees to let it go forward. Are you prepared to do that?" James asked.

The two looked at each other a little uneasily. They both knew that doing anything without Billy's support was not the best way to get ahead, but when they looked back at James they both nodded in agreement.

"If we don't do something this place is not going to survive. Someone is going to get hurt, or the competition is going to keep eating our lunch. Either way, something has to change," Sean added with determination.

With that settled, James went to see Billy. He had every intention of making it clear exactly what his expectations were. But when he arrived at Billy's office, Billy's assistant informed him that Billy had been called away from the plant and would not be returning that day. James, feeling highly annoyed, pulled out his notebook and under questions wrote, "How can you deliver defect elimination without executive leadership?" In the margin, he wrote gloomily, "You can't".

James spent the rest of the day working with the operator PM team and trying to leave follow-up notes for Sean, the HR head, and for the head of engineering about setting up teams and Defect Elimination Game workshops for the coming weeks.

James left later that afternoon in order to catch his flight back to Atlanta. He thanked everyone, exited the building with a sigh, and headed for his rental car.

"Jeez," he said out loud as he slid into the car and inserted his keys into the ignition. He pulled out of the parking lot as he mentally sorted through all of the information he needed to record in his notebook. Unfortunately, his thoughts became more and more pessimistic the closer he got to the airport. Billy sure hadn't been very cooperative. James sighed but decided to give Billy the benefit of the doubt. Perhaps he wasn't being fair to Billy. After all the man was obviously busy and spread too thin. He was probably just extremely busy, not uninterested, James reassured himself. He'd just hoped for a little bit more cooperation and enthusiasm. Was that too much to ask, he wondered? He decided that he'd gain Billy's support as the initiative picked up steam. He just needed to be patient and optimistic.

He had three more plants to meet with this month. He needed not only to get them all started on the program, but he'd be monitoring the results and mentoring site management all along the way. And at the same time, he'd be adding new plants into the mix on a weekly basis. If Houston was any indication of what he could expect, he knew he was in big trouble.

Chapter 13

IN WHICH THE TRUTH IS REVEALED

Billy snuck into the plant from the back parking lot after a day of off-site meetings he'd conveniently arranged for the week James Emery would be at his plant. He stood at the window in his office overlooking the front parking lot. He seethed with fury as he watched James pull out. As his car disappeared around the corner, Billy spun on his heel and stalked out of his office, slamming the door behind him. His secretary jumped at the sound and then cringed at the look of fury on his face as he stormed past her desk.

"Call my management team into the conference room, immediately!" he barked out as he rounded the fax machine and proceeded to stalk down the hall. The snarl on his face sent people in the hall scurrying to get out of his way, but he couldn't gather up enough calmness to care.

He was ticked off. No, he was furious! He couldn't believe the nerve of James Emery coming to his plant and telling him what to do and how to do it. He just couldn't stomach the thought of some stupid corporate flunky trying to manipulate him. His gut clenched with the thought of all that he'd put up with this week. His jaw ached from clenching his teeth every time he had held back his true feelings, or an insulting retort. He had been able to keep a tight rein on his anger, and he'd played the nice guy convincingly enough he hoped. But now that James was gone, it was time to explain to his management team just who was in charge here, and who would be making the final decisions when it came to his plant. The stupid initiatives that had been spewing out of James' mouth were just not going to take priority at his plant, if they happened at all. It was all just crap. He would bide his time until Corporate fixated on the next flavor of the month.

Billy marched into the conference room, pulled out a seat, and sat to wait impatiently for all of his managers to report. He looked down at his watch and wondered what his wife was making for dinner. This wouldn't take long, he thought. He'd lay down the law, spell it all out and then he was out of here for the weekend! He felt better already.

James' thoughts turned philosophical as he inched along the highway in afternoon rush hour traffic. James was proud that he'd successfully navigated the Heroic Change journey by transforming the Atlanta site.

Although Atlanta had just about met all their goals, he knew it was important to keep the momentum going. It would also be important to make sure the plant did not regress while his attention was diverted and his focus shifted to all the other sites he was now responsible for.

He'd thought that it would be easy to apply the lessons learned in Atlanta to all the other sites with the exact same success, perhaps, an even better, quicker success. But in that moment, it occurred to James that though he'd completed the Atlanta portion of the journey, just like a chambered nautilus who continually builds his house, his journey was not yet complete. He now realized that he was at the beginning of the next stage of his "Journey of Change". As he worked to transform the entire company of Modern Products Manufacturing into a world-class organization, his journey would continue along a long, lonely road of trials that would need to be overcome. He felt a shudder down his spine as he realized the enormity of the undertaking.

James realized that the MIT computer model was the best resource he had to tackle this task. There was no way they could have created the changes at Atlanta without the model to guide them and help them understand what was happening along the way. They never could have created The Defect Elimination Game without the model. And they could never have communicated so well with the workers without the game. He knew that this was the key to solving the problems he would encounter at the other sites.

James realized from his experience in Houston that the other sites would not easily adopt the activities that had been implemented at Atlanta. In fact, James hadn't copied what was done at St. Louis except through the interpretation of Chance. James reflected that each Hero Journey would have to be unique, and each site would probably have to reinvent the activities to match the situation they were facing. He now recognized that creating the *Hero Journey Manual* as a cookbook just wouldn't work. It would have to be more dynamic than that.

At least, he had Mark Sterman's model to help evaluate the culture that existed at each individual site in order to calculate the value that a culture change would bring to each of them. Since the MIT team had created a process to calibrate the model to each individual site, James would be able to provide some guidance on best practices throughout the journey. The key would be to use the model to avoid mistakes like those that were made with MRS. Dynamic Benchmarking might be a good name for the process, James thought. He knew he needed to get in touch with Mark Sterman.

He concentrated on his driving and merged into the exit lane to enter into the main entrance of the airport. As traffic into the airport thinned out, his thoughts turned back to work. What he really needed to model was the Hero's Journey itself in order to guide the social aspect of the journey. He'd read, *The Hero with A Thousand Faces*, as well as a few other books, about the Hero's Journey, and he now had a much better understanding of how everything that had happened to him mirrored a typical Hero's Journey. He knew that the Hero's Journey would be the key to helping all of the sites accomplish all the goals of the change effort.

After his visit with Billy, he now understood that his biggest challenge would be getting managers more involved and onboard. The Defect Elimination Game that MIT had created from their last model was instrumental in helping the workers to understand what kind of performance was possible, and how to set and achieve those goals. But managers were a tough nut to crack. They simply weren't learning the lessons as well as the workers, and that was a major obstacle that would need to be overcome. It was imperative that James understand and model the work of managers, and he knew that the new model would be vital to the forward momentum they were all hoping to achieve.

One of the managers had put it quite well when he said, "About all we can do is change the players and let them play the game."

The Defect Elimination Game did not allow anyone to change the players and watch them play. Managers needed to learn how to change the players when things weren't going well. James thought back to how he had actually changed the game in the field with the help of The Hero's Journey framework. It had helped him to know when it was time to let Vance go and fill the position with Steve, from the shadow network. James now understood how that move was key to the wildly successful change effort in Atlanta. James smiled as the seemingly endless possibilities sprang to mind.

Epilogue

James' Heroic Change journey continues. What will happen next? Will Atlanta continue to improve? Will Atlanta sustain the change? Will Atlanta regress while James' attention is focused on the other plants? And will James be successful in his company-wide change effort? All of these questions and more will be revealed in the next book of the Heroic Change series.

ADDITIONAL RESOURCES:

1. The Hero with a Thousand Faces by Joseph Campbell
2. Business Dynamics: Systems Thinking and Modeling for a Complex World by John Sterman (Pg. 66 - 78)
3. Awakening the Heroes Within by Carol S. Pearson
4. The Wisdom of Teams: Creating the High Performance Organization by Jon R. Katzenbach & Douglas K. Smith
5. The Breakthrough Strategy: Using Short-Term Successes to Build the High Performance Organization by Robert H. Schaffer
6. The Fifth Discipline: The Art and Practice of The Learning Organization by Peter Senge
7. The Fifth Discipline Fieldbook: Strategies and Tools for Building a Learning Organization by Peter Senge et al. (Pg. 550 - 553)
8. 5th Generation Management - Integrating Enterprises through Human Networking by Charles M. Savage
9. The Will to Meaning by Viktor E. Frankl
10. Kinds of Power by James Hillman
11. A New American TPM: Leadership Requirements for Breakthrough Change by James D. Griffith, Manufacturing Mgr. BP Amoco Chemicals, Green Lake, Texas, Donovan J. Kuenzli, Refinery General Manager Clark Oil, Port Arthur Texas, Paul A. Monus, Sr. Project Mananger, BP Amoco Chemicals, Lima Ohio - Presented at NPRA Maintenance Conference MC-99-95/May 27, 1999
12. Link to article: http://www.manufacturinggame.com/docs/ExecutiveSummaryNPRA99.pdf
13. Complexity and Creativity in Organizations by Ralph D. Stacey
14. Design for Evolution by Erich Jantsch
15. The Self Organizing Universe by Erich Jantsch
16. The Dance of Change: A Fifth Discipline Resource by Peter Senge, Art Kleiner, Charlotte Roberts, Richard Ross, George Roth & Bryan Smith (Chapter 5, page 174)
17. Theory of Constraints by Eliyahu M. Goldratt
18. RCM II: Reliability-Centered Maintenance by John Moubray
19. RCM: Gateway to World Class Maintenance by Anthony M. Smith, Glenn R. Hinchcliffe

20. The Age of Heretics by Art Kleiner
21. From Being to Becoming: Time and Complexity in the Physical Sciences by Ilya Prigogine
22. Order Out of Chaos by Ilya Prigogine
23. The End of Certainty by Ilya Prigogine
24. General System Theory: Foundations, Development Applications by Ludwig Von Bertalanffy
25. Spiral Up by Jane C. Linder (Chapter 2)
26. Making Common Sense Common Practice by Ron Moore
27. On Purposeful Systems by Russell L. Ackoff and Fred E. Emery
28. The Goal: A Process of Ongoing Improvement by Eliyahu M. Goldratt, Jeff Cox
29. Organizatonal Culture and Leadership by Edgar H. Schein
30. Organizational Psychology by Edgar H. Schein
31. The Dramatic Universe Volumes I – IV by J.G. Bennett
32. The Haystack Syndrome: Sifting Information out of The Data Ocean by Eliyahu M. Goldratt
33. Exploring Complexity by Gregoire Nicolis and Ilya Prigogine

Authors

Winston P. Ledet, *President*
Ledet Enterprises, Inc. / The Manufacturing Game®
Winston did his undergraduate work at the University of Southwestern Louisiana and received his Ph.D. in chemical engineering at the University of Texas in Austin. He has 27 years of experience with E.I. DuPont de Nemours serving in a variety of capacities in research, technical, works engineering, operations, human resources/safety, and maintenance. He is one of the creators of The Manufacturing Game®, which was created as part of his work at DuPont. Winston formed his consulting firm, Ledet Enterprises, Inc. using The Manufacturing Game® to drive improvement efforts in process industries and discreet parts manufacturing sites around the world. He has extensive capability in System Dynamics modeling, proactive manufacturing, and large-scale organizational change strategies. Ledet Enterprises, Inc. has developed and participated in the development of several other simulations since the early 1990's with a focus on improvement of safety and reliability through organizational culture change. Winston has worked with 168 companies in 26 countries, representing 13 different industries, all with the same goal in mind – improving reliability through sustainable heroic change.

Winston J. Ledet
Winston was one of the original contributors to the creation of The Manufacturing Game® in the early 1990's. During his years with Ledet Enterprises, Inc. he worked with over 40 companies on reliability improvement efforts in a variety of industries including petrochemicals, paper, automotive, mining and consumer goods manufacturing. He was previously an operations consultant with McKinsey & Co. He has been an adjunct professor of business dynamics at Emory's Goizueta Business School. He holds a masters in management science from MIT where he focused on operations management.

Sherri M. Abshire
As an employee of Ledet Enterprises, Inc., Sherri works closely with Winston P. Ledet on numerous writing, research and development projects. When not working at Ledet, Sherri volunteers her time teaching Junior Achievement programs at local schools and enjoys reading, traveling with her Expat husband, and Sunday drives to deliver care packages to her daughter, a Texas A&M Aggie.

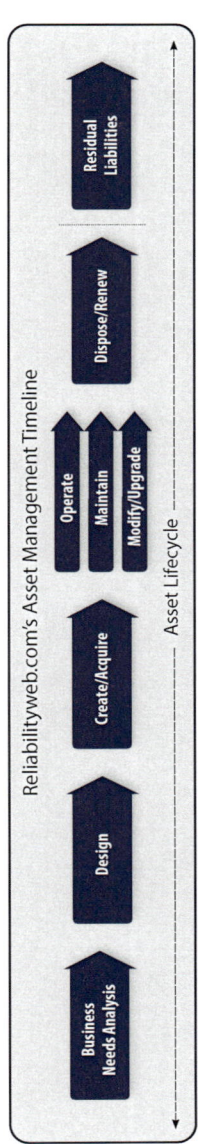

ABOUT RELIABILITYWEB.COM

Created in 1999, Reliabilityweb.com provides educational information and peer-to-peer networking opportunities that enable safe and effective reliability and asset management for organizations around the world.

ACTIVITIES INCLUDE:

Reliabilityweb.com® (www.reliabilityweb.com) includes educational articles, tips, video presentations, an industry event calendar and industry news. Updates are available through free email subscriptions and RSS feeds. **Confiabilidad.net** is a mirror site that is available in Spanish at www.confiabilidad.net.

Uptime® Magazine (www.uptimemagazine.com) is a monthly magazine launched in 2005 that is highly prized by the reliability and asset management community.

Reliability Leadership Institute® Conferences and Training Events (www.reliabilityleadership.com) offer events that range from unique, focused-training workshops and seminars to small focused conferences to large industry-wide events, including the International Maintenance Conference (IMC), MaximoWorld and The RELIABILITY Conference™ (TRC).

MRO-Zone Bookstore (www.mro-zone.com) is an online bookstore offering a reliability and asset management focused library of books, DVDs and CDs published by Reliabilityweb.com.

Association of Asset Management Professionals (www.maintenance.org) is a member organization and online community that encourages professional development and certification and supports information exchange and learning with 50,000+ members worldwide.

A Word About Social Good

Reliabilityweb.com is mission-driven to deliver value and social good to the reliability and asset management communities. *Doing good work and making profit is not inconsistent*, and as a result of Reliabilityweb.com's mission-driven focus, financial stability and success has been the outcome. For over a decade, Reliabilityweb.com's positive contributions and commitment to the reliability and asset management communities have been unmatched.

Other Causes

Reliabilityweb.com has financially contributed to include industry associations, such as SMRP, AFE, STLE, ASME and ASTM, and community charities, including the Salvation Army, American Red Cross, Wounded Warrior Project, Paralyzed Veterans of America and the Autism Society of America. In addition, we are proud supporters of our U.S. Troops and first responders who protect our freedoms and way of life. That is only possible by being a for-profit company that pays taxes.

I hope you will get involved with and explore the many resources that are available to you through the Reliabilityweb.com network.

Warmest regards,
Terrence O'Hanlon
CEO, Reliabilityweb.com

Reliabilityweb.com®, Uptime®, The RELIABILITY Conference™, MaximoWorld and Reliability Leadership Institute® are the trademarks or registered trademarks of Reliabilityweb.com and its affiliates in the USA and in several other countries.